Jimmy Leggett re

A Boyhood in the Fleggs

Articles written for
Clippesby Parish News and Views
and collected for publication by
Pauline Willmott
who also did the drawings

Larks Press

Published by The Larks Press
Ordnance Farmhouse
Guist Bottom, Dereham NR20 5PF

01328 829207

Larks.Press@btinternet.com

www.booksatlarkspress.co.uk

Printed by C.L.E.
St Ives, Cambridgeshire

British Library Cataloguing-in-Publication Data
A catalogue record for this book is available
from the British Library

No part of this book, text or illustrations, may be reproduced in any way without the prior permission of the publisher and the copyright holders.

The photograph on page 6 appeared in the book, *Finest Hour*
by Phil Craig and Tim Clayton (BBC Publications: 1999)
and in theTV film of the same name.

All profit from the sale of this book will be donated to Clippesby Church

© Text – Sandra DeVille Leggett
Drawings - Pauline Willmott

ISBN 978 1 904006 57 2

FOREWORD

I am proud to have the honour of writing the foreword to this delightful collection of articles and illustrations that were written for the *Parish News and Views* twenty or more years ago.

My Father loved writing of his experiences of boyhood and beyond and would usually delegate me as one of his proof-readers. He was always so modest and unassuming regarding his writing. The article for any particular month would be presented to me for scrutiny in an A4 envelope previously used as, of course, would be the paper it was written on. Dad hated waste of any kind and would write on the back of most correspondence! The little boy who brought a rabbit skin in lieu of payment for entry into the 'flicks' couldn't be expected to use pristine new paper for his messages!

Ernest James Leggett was born in the small, scattered hamlet of Clippesby near Great Yarmouth on December 22nd 1919. Even though he had been christened Ernest he was to my knowledge mostly known by his family as Jimmy or The Boy Jimma.

I remember him telling about the family moving from Weston Longville, which is also in Norfolk, to their house on Low Road in Clippesby. As people were fond of saying in those days 'New house new baby' so it was here that young Jimmy was born and spent his early life.

My grandfather was a farm labourer and times were hard for him as for many others in the years between the two world wars. Tragedy had struck the family when Uncle Freddie, my father's brother, had been crippled in a freak accident when out playing with his sister and a friend. The little lad managed to crawl home and was put to bed. He never walked again. He was nine years old.*

It was five years after the accident that Jimmy was born; the two boys were very close friends. It was Uncle Freddie who instilled in my father patience and a love of the countryside. He also taught him how to shoot a rifle, which was to prove very useful when he joined the Army.

Young Jimmy went to the village school at Fleggburgh, a daily walk of about three miles, which he and the other village children had to do in all weathers; they would sometimes arrive cold and wet for the start of school and have to stay in those same clothes all day long.

Jimmy was, I'm sure, like most boys of his age, lively and not averse to

*See Postscript, p.178

3

planning the odd prank or two but he excelled at school, especially in English literature, and he loved sports and the countryside. Unfortunately when he eventually won a scholarship at eleven to qualify for the Grammar School he was unable to go because my grandparents could not afford the uniform. So he had no choice but to stay on at the village school and leave at fourteen years old – as did thousands of other young people at that time – and try to find a job in an unwelcome environment.

I am convinced that had my father benefited from a better education he would have been a successful journalist or writer of some sort, but as it was, work was hard to find and so, in 1935 at the age of fifteen my father joined the Second Battalion of the Royal Norfolk Regiment on boy service; it was to change his life completely.

As well as learning infantry drill the boy soldiers were trained as bandsmen. Dad loved his leopard-skin and drum; he also excelled at playing the bugle and in later life he continued with this playing for Remembrance services and military gatherings. The shooting skills he learnt at an early age now bore fruit as he gained marksman's badges for both rifle and Bren light machine gun. This had the bonus of extra pay, which, of course, pleased my father enormously.

After three happy years in the Army, training in England and in Gibraltar, war was declared and the young Ernie, as he was now known, found himself embroiled in bitter and heavy fighting on the Franco/Belgian border. Whilst defending a position on the banks of the river Escaut he was seriously wounded and eventually evacuated from the beaches of Dunkirk.

He wrote movingly of that particular episode in his life when he was Editor of the *Dunkirk Veterans' Journal*. 'My thoughts constantly stray to the time I was located and picked up by the stretcher-bearers, transported to the Forward Casualty Clearing Station, thence to a hospital train and ambulances. I owe a tremendous debt to the S.B.s, the M.O. and a Belgian nurse, the R.E.s in charge of the train and the R.A.M.C. orderlies on board, the R.A.S.C. ambulance drivers, and, on being placed amongst the sand dunes at Dunkirk, for those unknown to me who covered me with their own bodies when danger threatened, and this was almost incessant.

I was twenty years of age, battered and broken, unable to defend myself and completely helpless, this is why I remember Dunkirk and the reason it means so much to me; it was the main part of my early life. The lifeblood which I shed will remain a part of France and Belgium for all time.'

The young Ernie was eventually safely transported to Newhaven and then to a hospital in Sussex. It wasn't till he was in his late seventies that my father told me of my grandmother visiting him in the hospital with his then fiancée. They had been told he would never walk again. Presumably at sight of the wheelchair by the bed the young lady decided to terminate the engagement.

Luck hadn't deserted my father entirely though and he met and married my mother Lucy in 1948 and had three children. By that time he had completed his Army service, ending up as a Military Policeman. Upon leaving the forces he joined the civilian Police Force. Dad was, in modern parlance, 'sartorially challenged', but as he said he'd been in uniform of one kind or another nearly all his life.

As time went on Dad became involved with the Dunkirk Veterans and was an active and productive member with many responsibilities including editing the Journal, which had a worldwide distribution. He enjoyed his work enormously and was very conscientious, never missing a deadline for the Journal or the parish magazine even when his health was failing.

When I moved to Clippesby in 1981 Dad became an active and worshipping member of our church community. He would gaze up at the same stained glass window with the crossed keys of St Peter that had fascinated him as a small boy so long ago. The crossed keys had been the insignia of the Royal Norfolks and he believed them to be an omen that he would survive and come home.

The Boy Jimma was finally laid to rest on a cold February day in 2001, in the beautiful churchyard of St Peter's at Clippesby, where, amongst the birdsong and wild flowers, I know he is fully at peace with his Lord. For the little drummer boy Reveille has sounded and he has gone to the last Parade Ground in the sky. I like to imagine him with his comrades and loved ones. I know he would be surprised but delighted to discover that his recollections of a bygone rural age would still be relevant and interesting to another generation.

Sandra DeVille Leggett

Jimmy Leggett as drummer, North Front, Gibraltar, 1938

CONTENTS

IN THE COUNTRYSIDE

The Countryside in Early Spring

Did we not consider ourselves exceptionally fortunate in February and also into March that year, in which period the weather treated us very favourably? During my young days in the 1920s I can remember little else than exceptionally cold winds, ice, snow and heavy rains, mostly during February and into March. Walking home from school at this time the darkness was imminent, and from the sky we heard the loud cawing and chattering of rooks and crows in their large and noisy gatherings, who, after their hard day of foraging for food, would be returning home to roost before settling down for the night in the rookery situated between Hall Farm and High House Farm. We would watch as they wheeled, whirled and dipped, and tumbled as in a state of turmoil, as the blackening clouds scudded across an already storm-threatened sky.

Smaller birds would be scurrying away making their beds in the thick hedgerows and ivy-strewn tree trunks. And someone, somewhere, would be saying, 'Looks like we're in for a rough old night.'

And so it always turned out to be, with the wind whistling and howling around the corners of the house, with rain lashing windows, doors and roofs, and the chimney pots moaning and groaning. Tucked away in bed, somehow I always found it soothed me off to sleep, but hoping, of course, that it would subside and calm down before I ventured off to school on the morrow. I imagine that most of my age-group are reminded of the chant we voiced at the time,

> *'The North wind doth blow, and we shall have snow;*
> *what will the robin do then, poor thing?'*

However, in the lanes, hedgerows and woods, spring had awakened, and we gathered catkins, from the various willows, alders and black poplars. Also, beds of white and purple violets would be budding up in the ditches and shady parts of the plantations, and in the beginning of April there would be masses of pale yellow primroses, and our respective mothers would be overwhelmed with bunches of wild flowers. The spectacular sight I enjoyed most, and still do welcome its arrival each year, is the snowy white blossom of the 'marrabellum', the yellow and red plum growing wild and commonly referred to as the 'marrabella'. At Ashby Hall Farm owned by Mr Wm. Molineux and later Major Frank Molineux, the hedges around each field were grown to a height of twelve to fifteen feet, and dotted amongst the thorn would be the odd 'marrabella' and at harvest time would be ripe to perfection. Oh, boy! the tummy aches and pains we suffered!

Some birds had already started to think about producing families, amongst which would be the sparrow, starling, wren, rook, blackbird, robin and thrush, and nest-building could be seen taking shape. If on a Saturday the weather was favourable, a day across the marshes, jumping over the dykes and searching for signs of water hens building their nests, would keep us out of other mischief, but in many places we would sink into the mud, disturbing the marsh gas (methane) and as it bubbled up we could detect the obnoxious smell it would produce. On arriving home one would be in trouble because little did we realize it but in fact we smelled like nothing on earth!

More of the Countryside in Spring

During the early 1920s and approaching the middle of April and into early May we noticed the grassy banks beside road ditches were massed with pale yellow primroses with red and white campions ready to burst from buds. On the marshes and damp meadows one could discern the beautiful thick-stemmed, heavy-leafed marsh marigold, with its glistening deep yellow petals, most conspicuous whilst vying with the cowslip and cuckoo flower. This was my favourite marsh flower, and whilst writing essays at school, I would often refer to it as the 'Queen of the Marsh'. We would gather huge bunches of primroses and later divide them into small bouquets, and during Sunday afternoon would offer them at 2d each from trays to the people in motor cars passing through to the coast. During the season most of us collected quite a few shillings to swell our money boxes.

On some bright sunny days butterflies, breeze-blown, scurrying and dancing, were in evidence and we would chase the painted ladies, peacocks, brimstone and the large garden white with its black spots and black edging to the wings. A trip to the corner plantations at the top road entrance to Hall Road would benefit us to the extent of large bunches of bluebells to keep in mother's favourable esteem.

Also at this time of year one of the favourite pastimes was collecting birds' eggs, and most of us had a large collection of most bird species. I have often climbed the very tall trees in the rookery which is situated to the south of the main road between Hall Farm and High House Farm, Billockby. In a slight breeze it was most exhilarating to be swaying with the topmost branches perhaps 90 feet high, and although a rook or crow's nest does not look exceptionally large from the ground, once up aloft in the tree tops, they turned out to be really massive piles of closely-woven sticks. When the eggs were obtained, usually one or two from a nest, they were carefully dropped through the branches into a school cap held by a friend.

Probably some readers who have been to the church at Billockby have noticed the holes which penetrate the remaining structure of the church tower. In my young days jackdaws would build their nests in these, and besides collecting eggs, many a household in the village would be sporting a tame jackdaw, which would eventually return to the wild. However, regarding the collection of eggs, and before I am severely castigated on our

next meeting, let me assure all of our readers that at this time there were thousands of each species, most of which nested in the hedgerows – also bear in mind that every field of five to ten acres or so was surrounded by a thick hedge and raised bank. There were also many more trees and plantations than there are now. I mentioned last month the tall hedges around the fields at Ashby Hall Farm. I imagine if at the time they were placed in a straight line they would cover the distance from Ashby to Fleggburgh, so you can envisage there was no need to legislate in law on the taking of eggs.

About this time of year the wooden spinning top was in favour. There were high flyers shaped similar to a mushroom with a hobnail inserted at the toe which when whipped would hum, dance and jump along the road, and during the early evenings the bottom road at Clippesby was alive with children whipping their tops. Of course, and as always, there were accidents as sometimes the whip would knot around the top, which would, 'of all the luck', send it into a window. I was constantly paying to replace window panes which fortunately in these times were only about 6d per square foot, but in the end I hit upon a very bright idea – why not have two tops, one being whipped and the other tucked away in the pocket? I did this and it proved to be a brainwave, and when the 'tinkling' occurred I was engrossed in savagely thrashing my substitute top, and when I was tackled, said, 'Oh, no, Mrs, it wasn't me!' But I did not get away with it; my mother was wise, and later, when going indoors, I received what is known in Norfolk as a

13

'thorough good soolen' or sometimes a good 'twilten'. I never could differentiate between them but they both hurt.

As still happens at this time of year, after a little heat during the day there started to build up over the fields and marshes a sultry and hazy mist which partly obliterated the myriad friendly shapes of trees and bushes and other objects to which we were accustomed during the day. The cattle on the meadows and marshes took on a grotesque form, and like all youngsters, when fantasies run wild, they just had to be ghosts and 'hikey-sprites', and it only needed a bullock to cough or the unexpected screech of an owl to send us indoors, wide-eyed and frightened.

However, although there are wild flowers blossoming in profusion, shrubs and trees in brilliant array, birds nesting and some with fledglings, there will occasionally be rain-storms with cold winds, and frost. During the early evening, after a fine day, you will probably encounter wisps of mist which arise and hover in the air like smoke, and drift out of reach – so do not forget the old warnings: 'Change not a clout till May be out,' and, 'Who doffs his coat on a winter's day will gladly put it on in May.'

The Oak-apple Ink

Again during the middle 1920s about the middle of May and into early June one noticed the hosts of lovely bluebells, red and white campion abounding in the woods and alongside hedgerows, whilst on the road banks and grass verges there was a more than large accumulation of white hemlock which when bruised or struck with a stick gave off a powerful obnoxious smell. Nevertheless their white spangled heads do in fact produce a novel flower bouquet and they with hawthorn blossom are shown to great effect in Clippesby Church when arranged by Jean. Also alongside ditches and under hedges we saw beautiful wild arum which we all knew as the familiar cuckoo pint or lords and ladies. On the commons and rough ground, yellow gorse and broom together with purple fox-gloves transformed the bareness of the landscape, and bees, in company with butterflies and day moths, supped greedily from these and red and white clovers, and with a mixture of honeysuckle, dandelion, clumps of daisy and numerous other species of flower they would fly away in an unsteady flight of wavering drunkenness, heavy with nectar and pollen.

How many readers remember that year after year we gathered oak-apples, which are now unobtainable, risking one's neck climbing along the branches of oak trees, took them home and, after the laborious task of boiling and stirring, waited for that magic ink which never became a reality, and yet we never tired in our efforts to beat the greatest leg-pull of our younger age.

I also remember very vividly how during the long light evenings most of the boys and young men of Clippesby and Billockby would assemble on the stretch of narrow marsh just off Billockby corner, which sufficed for our cricket pitch. The narrow track situated between the plantation and the dyke was an ideal spot, with the stumps cut from nut-wood and set up on the road end, and with a single marker at the other end we played until darkness fell. Our bat would be cut and fashioned from a wooden paling taken off someone's garden fence. Hitting a ball into the plantation was out, and likewise into the dyke, but over the dyke and into the adjoining field was a sixer. It was fine whilst batting, but fielding had us eaten up by gnats and those other little insects which hovered in spiral swarms and which we referred to as 'mingens'.

On most days, whilst the sun was bearing down, it warmed the water in the dykes but later on while the first touch of chill rode the night air, wisps of mist arose like wood smoke and drifted past on an imperceptible breeze. This was the time to draw stumps and prepare for home. On the way the sweetness of the many blossoms and tree foliage filled the late evening with a pleasant aroma of subtle scents in which only country folk could indulge. Motor vehicles were scarce, as were the steam locomotives, so no sudden inrush of air disturbed those aromatic pleasures. This was fine until reaching the next farm manure heap, also steaming and emitting a slightly foreign flavour, but one to which we had grown accustomed.

The road surfaces in those days were mostly of gravel chippings on tar and every two or three years the Acle causeway and bottom roads were resurfaced. Tar in barrels, left by the verges would signal the tar gangs. The tar would be heated in a large copper type container with a fire box underneath to which were fitted three iron wheels, one of which was mounted on a turntable to which was affixed a long iron draw bar enabling it to be pulled along. The hot tar was run off from a tap into galvanised watering cans and thence to the road and the chippings then spread evenly over the surface by men using shovels. Even after being rolled down by a steam roller the whole project was a messy affair and remained so for several days after.

Among the paraphernalia of the tar gang was a water-sprayer equipped with a large tank supported on large iron wheels, a pump operated by a hand lever and an attached hose to facilitate filling. Shafts were fitted to the chassis within which a horse was harnessed. A seat was fitted to the top of the tank and a foot pedal, when pressed downward, would allow a flush of water from a spray bar behind the tank. Fancy leaving this implement near the plantation. It was too good to be true, as about six of us could pull it along easily and after filling the tank with water from the 'longspring' which is the dyke running alongside the main road, we would go up and down spraying the roads. We also knew that the policeman always approached from Fleggburgh or Thurne direction and lookouts were posted to signal if the PC Lambert of the day was seen. Had he passed along our way I wonder what his reactions would have been when he saw the wet roads. We had fun and enjoyed ourselves but none of the equipment or plant was broken or vandalised.

On other occasions we would frequent the marshes with our stout ash dyke-jumping poles. These were supple and anything up to eight or nine feet in length which enabled us to cross from marsh to marsh by vaulting the wider dykes without having to find and use the 'liggers' placed across them and used by marshmen and farmers. The main objective was to place the pole in the middle of the dyke and then with a jump from the side the motion would propel one to the other side. This was great fun and we enjoyed ourselves immensely but as always mishaps do occur and on occasions, as weight was applied to the pole, it sunk into the soft mud and one would finish up in the water. Those readers who are acquainted with marsh dykes will know that being covered in duckweed and other rotting vegetation does not improve upon the normal and usual rustic smells of a country schoolboy. Sometimes without knowing it we had collected one or more of those black slug-like water creatures which attached themselves to our skins like the leeches they were. However, to compensate for our misfortunes we would collect several eggs from the nests of water hens which, like the watercress gathered from the less stagnant waters, were delicious when eaten.

At this time of year the Acle causeway to St Margaret's Mill was a sight to behold, each grass verge being shaded by a continuous line of willow trees in full leaf and a wide swathe of vegetation which appeared as a sheet of brilliant yellow on a carpet of waving green rushes. These were the beautiful wild iris or yellow flag, and they would be plucked carefully to decorate many a home. Its leaves are sharp-edged and sword-shaped and can severely cut if not handled properly. On the marsh side of the 'longspring' generous spreads of cowslips and silverweed would vie with other wild flowers to beautify this corner of Norfolk but, alas, not so today as in these modern times of advanced agriculture the great majority have disappeared. I only wish, in retrospect, I had appreciated the glorious vistas of colour much more than I did. Our modern and present generation is missing a great deal and cannot ever become aware of the countryside nature as I did.

The Marshes Lush and Green

Some of the older generation who relished the magnificent sights of the past when traversing from Billockby corner to the once well-known Hermitage Inn, where the marshes on either side of the road terminated at Acle, then enjoyed the countryside at its best. The road was lined on either side with willow trees, set about six feet apart, and when one succumbed to the rigours of life it was immediately replaced with a young sapling and never was there a space left unfilled. It was said at the time that the roots from either side spread under the road surface and embraced and entwined like nature's lovers to strengthen and stabilize the road. Every two years or so the vigorous branches were cut off close to the crown of the trunk and every gardener and allotment holder would then replenish his stock of pea sticks as it was then the custom to grow the tall variety of garden peas and in addition almost every household sported a tall row of fragrant sweet pea. A good-sized bunch of these pea sticks would cost the purchaser one old 6d coin and would be transported home shoulder high with one or two stops on the way for a 'spit and a draw.'

Behind the willow trees ran the 'deeks', always filled with water which kept the roots supple, and on the other side stretched that green and pleasant expanse of nature's glory as far as and even beyond the river. On each side cattle grazed and roamed peacefully at will in proportionate numbers and I remember occasions when I was cajoled into taking a quart bottle to the 'Jug and Bottle' at the Bridge Inn, Acle, to fetch old ale for my grandfather and father. At this time a young person could, in law, carry home a corked and sealed receptacle and the licensee was obliged to see that this was done, but on the way home I very often broke the seal and had one or two swigs and by the time I reached the last marsh at Clippesby and glanced across the distance I often wondered where all the extra numbers of cattle had come from – I saw ten times as many. On arriving home no-one noticed I had undone the seal; at least they appeared not to have done as I pulled off that which remained from the neck of the bottle.

In later life the same law applied and I saw many a young lad eagerly running the same errand as I had done many years before and on checking found the seal to be broken but remembering my own little misdeeds I became a sympathetic compatriot of Lord Nelson.

However, during the latter years I have noticed the marshes being ploughed over and in place of grass and golden buttercups corn now flourishes and ripples in waves when brushed by a kind and gentle breeze. Cattle numbers have diminished drastically but this is shortly destined to change. Although still under the cloak of intense secrecy I risk the scepticism of your get-together talks, whether it be after church, village gatherings, Mothers' Unions or Women's Institutes, when I tell you, in strict confidence of course, that once again and very shortly, the marshes will be transferred back to their original use.

On your next journey to Acle or Norwich, just before approaching the small turning on the left which takes one to Stokesby, when the air intake inside your car sets about a tingling nostril sensation savouring the essence of long and well-worn socks, don't despair because you have just discovered the latest development in a new Broadland enterprise – CHEESE!

Still in its infancy, a small and inconspicuous building sheltering alongside the river bank, by using milk transported over from the Channel Isles and taking curd – the coagulated part of the milk – has given rise to the most delicious cheese one could ever want to dream of. It resembles, in taste, a delicious combination of stilton, blue vein, cheddar and cottage cream and is completely encased in the round shape of the very familiar

Dutch cheese with the red waxed outer skin. But, unlike the Dutch variety, which needs to be skinned, our cheese so adeptly named 'Norfolk Broadland Golden Buttercup,' is coated with an eatable substance of vegetable protein crust. Unlike other cheeses which are stored to maturity sitting in line on racks in ventilated sheds, the 'Golden Buttercup' brand is brought to maturity out in the open air attached to conveyer lines hung high over the marshes and if you care to glance to your left on passing the Stokesby turn you will see them just about thirty yards away in line with the road, high enough to prevent theft and to curtail the evil thoughts of 'nickers' but not too high to fully benefit from the ozone and various penetrating essences essential for their subtle and titillating flavour.

At Acle river bridge you will notice they disappear underground to emerge and rise again on the marsh at the other side for some distance. Their golden-yellow appearance is very pleasing to the eye of a cheese person.

Permission is being sought to install more conveyer lines on both sides of the river and shortly, small Co-ops are to be formed within which anyone owning small parcels of land can, with the assistance of others, accommodate two or more Jersey cows and it is hoped many people in the area will take part in this lucrative and worthwhile venture.

Holiday-makers will suffice for all the advertising needed to be done, and on taking camera shots of the dewy-eyed animals with their long

fluttering eyelashes, will say to their friends and relatives far and wide, 'These are the beautiful creatures that supply the cream ingredients for Golden Buttercup.'

Hanging aloft, they are unaffected by frost, rain, mist, wind and other elements but you will be bound to notice they are kept well apart; this is because bruising does in fact ruin the fine texture. Why, you may well ask, and full marks for doing so, are they not ravaged and pecked to pieces by them 'little old badds' especially 'them there blinkin' old crows,' but there lies the ingenious modern secret – the hanging cheese-protector alarm – an innovation known as the 'cheese bug' and no bigger than the minutest watch battery inserted just under the crown and which emits a piercing wail and scares the living daylights out of everything approaching within two feet. Even when being harvested by the 'removers' as they are termed to be, 'lug muffs' have to be worn.

No longer need East Anglians flock down to Cheddar Gorge in Somerset for a sniff of cheese and to savour the aroma; it is now on their own doorstep, so to speak. We have had the era of 'Bu-tiful Norfolk tarkeys' and now comes the next explosive moment with the sensational: Let's show Europe the way with our 'Golden Buttercups.'

The rinsed over and then eatable skins, no thicker than that of a 'gnat's winter waistcoat', glow in the darkness when mature and the occupants of mystery tour coaches will be elated to see them ripen on the high wires – 'That one's ready!' 'Coo, look at that. There's another one!'

It is a picturesque scene even now, enhancing the expectation of a much-needed and brighter panorama but when summer is in full bloom and the river is busy with its flow of holiday traffic, wildlife of all types in immediate sight, the cheeses maturing aloft with their benefactors – the beautiful Jersey cows underneath – surely this will be one corner of our be-littered island which will be referred to as the 'Garden of East Anglia.'

I have good tidings; before the first batches arrive in the delicatessens, I have been promised six of the best for mouthwatering test-tasting at the next harvest festival supper at Clippesby Club House. You lucky people!

E. J. Leggpull
29th March 1991. (Are you sure it wasn't April 1st, Jimmy? – Ed.)

The Old-time Harvest

In the 1920s by the middle of July all the hay had been gathered in and stacked for winter fodder, and sometimes I was lucky enough to ride on top of the last load from the marsh to the farm, holding grimly on to a two-tined fork stuck well down into the load, and also holding firmly to the binding rope.

Following the haymaking, the hedges and banks would be trimmed ready for the main farming event of the year – harvest. We would be on holiday from school by this time and would watch the men with scythes cut a passage around the outside perimeter of a corn field to give a clear way for the horses pulling the 'binder'. This was the time for action, when the boys of the village resorted to the plantation to cut ourselves a harvest cudgel with the largest knob on the end that we could find, to chase and stop the rabbits escaping. In those days these were in large numbers and considered as a great pest to the farmer, and this was one occasion when their numbers could be curtailed. The binder would commence cutting the outside of the field and slowly and gradually work towards the middle; consequently the rabbits moved into the small area of standing corn remaining. Mostly everyone in the village would gather for this moment, after which the rabbits were shared out, and believe me, the harvest bunny was a succulent addition to the family diet during this period. Although the boys chased and saw off the greater number of rabbits, they didn't always receive one as due recompense, and many a time one would be hidden under a 'shoof' at the edge of the field for later collection.

Following the cutting, the 'shooves', which had been cut and tied and deposited by the binder, would then be stood up in 'shoks' of eight or more to assist in final drying and to ripen the corn. This procedure followed after the cutting of every cornfield on the farm, until completed.

Close to the farm, a stackyard would be selected where for the produce of each field a stack would be built, commencing by laying a bottom comprised of hedge and bank trimmings. I revelled in this part of harvest because I then became that which was known as a 'holdgee' boy, which meant that I rode the horse pulling the wagon which was being loaded with 'shooves' from the 'shoks'. The horse and wagon would be moved between the rows of 'shoks' and when the last 'shoof' was being hoisted up to the loader I would holler, 'Hold Gee!' to give warning to hold tight. When loaded the wagon would be taken to the stack and an empty one taken back to the field.

During this time the men would work continuously through the day and then at four o'clock in the afternoon usually the entire family gathered in the field for 'fourses'. There would be the pleasant aroma of steaming hot meat puddings accompanied by fresh peas, carrots and beans, just pulled from the garden. They even went as far as apple or raspberry pie and custard for 'arters'. This procedure would continue daily, except for Sunday, for as long as it took, but was mostly completed before the end of August, taking roughly about five weeks from start to finish, when in the stackyard there would be anything up to ten or twelve massive stacks standing like the hulls of huge ships.

There were times of course when one would get a sudden feeling of coldness in the air, and glancing up to the sky, would see dark clouds gathering over 'Will's Mother's', and subsequently hear the distant roll of thunder and see the frightening forked lightning rip the sky apart. Before the downpour one could feel that breathlessness which precedes every storm, when the air becomes chill but clammy, and the quietness of nature tends to become unbearable, somewhat akin to those moments before a battle is to commence, but when unleashed is taken in one's stride. These storms would call a halt to harvest until the following day.

Once the stacks were standing, and the fields bereft of their golden produce, the stacks had to be thatched to protect them from the gales and

ravages of winter, plus the pernicious attention of the crows and rooks. This was professional work, and one in which my father was most capable, and probably for the whole of September he would be thatching, using wheat straw from a previous harvest, and using 'brotches' and 'binder twine' to secure a steadfast and watertight thatch. There they would stand the rigours of winter, until probably in the New Year, when the price was suitable, or 'the farmer wanted a new bike', along came the threshing tackle to do its worst and leave a gap on the skyline – but we now had a soft straw stack on which to play!

The main kill-joys of such a pleasant and healthy boyhood during harvest were the incessant invasions of flies, which drove us almost mad, and the super-extra stinginess of the nettle, which was soothed by the ever-useful dock leaf – and come to think of it, it had other uses as well! I also remember, as no doubt will several other readers, suddenly jumping high in the air, having been stung by a horse fly, and watching a big red bump gradually grow on the affected part. If these things caused cattle to bolt and run amok, just think of the pain it caused to a small boy!

But never mind, charged with extra exuberance and with a yen for a 'bit more larnin' ', we'd be off to school again and not long hence would be chanting, 'Christmas is coming, the geese are getting fat, please put a penny in the old man's hat!'

The Acorn Pop-gun

Another 1920s harvest is over and done with, and on the approach to many a farm premises huge corn stacks now dominate the skyline of the countryside, resembling the huge hulls of ships berthed and lying at anchor in a harbour. The extra money earned during almost dawn to dusk labours has been spent, and it is most noticeably obvious how many of the youngsters from larger families walk with pride, wearing their new boots, and have discarded the long jacket or coat which concealed the sitting down portion of short trousers where recently the tail end of a shirt was evident and a patch was again flapping. Readers of my age will not have to ponder long on how extremely hard these times could be for some, in the so-called good old days, and will doubtless immediately recapture the expression voiced regarding this chilly embarrassment.

Then again I am positive many older readers can recall the repetitive occasions when a large hole sudden appeared in the heel of a sock caused by the slouching effect of oversize hand-me-down footwear. 'You've got a bit potato showing,' someone would cruelly point out, and to hide the offending part one would pull the toe of the sock over and under the tootsies, thus covering the gaping heel section under the sole of the foot, but suffering infinite discomfort all day through having a huge rolled lump under the toes, and some blisters into the bargain when arriving home from school.

I remember how, on one occasion this happened to me, I took my socks off completely and sure enough whilst in class my teacher, Mrs. Bracey, with her eagle eyes spotted something amiss. 'James, where are your socks?'

'Sorry, miss, I got a hole in the heel so I took 'em off!' I answered sheepishly.

Then I got a right ticking off. 'Don't say 'em, boy – it is them! – them! – them! Stay in during playtime and write 'THEM' one hundred times!'

Couldn't win, could we, for not 'torken' proper!

Foolishly I retaliated with 'That 'ent fair!' and painfully thought to myself – 'Stone the crows, I'm in for it now.'

With that determinant withering look which teachers have, she said, 'Also a hundred lines of That IS NOT fair.' I opened my mouth again but with a look in her eyes as if to imply – you just dare say it – I kept silent. It took me two play periods to complete my lines, after which, with a smug grin on my face I took them to her. On my departing from the classroom she called, 'James!'

'Yes, miss?'

'Don't you dare let the air from my bicycle tyres!' This hurt me, as I had only intended to give the back wheel a good kick.

Straw stubble left in the fields and resembling a rough haircut would now be scaled off with a cutting ploughshare followed by a cultivator and chain harrow, after which, with drying winds, one would see the spear grass, couch and bindweed and other rubbish being piled into heaps. When dry, and on a favourable day, one heap was put to flame and a worker could be seen running between each heap carrying lighted material on a fork until each pile was burnt out.

Soon after, the plough would be in daily use, with the old-type single share plough drawn by two horses and steered by the ploughman traversing up and down continuously all day long and being mobbed by scores of raucous, ravenous seagulls gorging themselves on the fat worms being hoisted to the surface.

How utterly tedious ploughing must have been! Can you imagine yourselves in the heavy leather boots with rows of metal studs and hobnails hammered into the soles, which all farm workers wore, and continually plodding to and fro, whilst ploughing a ten-acre field cutting a furrow of, I think, about twelve inches, or in modern parlance, 304 mm. Averaging two acres each day you would be walking behind the plough, hauling and pulling the handles to keep a straight line, for a distance of 16½ miles, give or take a point per cent each way. Every so often you would stop for a couple of minutes to have a swig of cold sugarless and milkless tea from a two pint bottle, and before commencing again would fill up and light a pipe with that obnoxious and odious-smelling weed they called shag tobacco. Those of you who, like myself, feel compassion for working animals, must also give a thought for the horses striding out the same distance, but in addition having to pull the ploughshare through the heavy clay soil; this could well sum up the old adage at the end of the day, 'As tired as a horse.'

Come dinner time how about sitting on a sack on a bank or in a 'holl', eating your gourmet meal – a chunk of bread in the left hand with a hunk of cheese held down on top of the bread with a thumb, plus a raw onion also held down on the bread, and cutting each with a 'shut' knife, the blade of which was also used for a myriad of day-to-day uses, two of which were cleaning out the bowl of the odious tobacco pipe and 'hulking' a rabbit.

However, I digress from my main subject. Whilst harvest was in progress we boys were scrutinising the oak trees to find the best crop of acorns in readiness for the pop-gun season. Also keen eyes were searching the hedgerows and copses for the thickest stemmed elder bushes, for now was the time to cut a thick-stemmed elder, shorten it to eight or nine inches, after which the white pith was removed from the core and behold this was the gun barrel. A length of soft wood usually obtained off an orange box was shaped and rounded off as a plunger leaving at least two inches of wide butt at one end. The toe end was wetted and banged against a wall until a washer was formed which when pushed into the barrel finished about an inch from the aperture. It was determined to be an efficient washer when by covering the end of the barrel with a thumb and withdrawing the plunger sharply there would be a resounding THUNK. An acorn bitten in half, placed into the breach, pushed up to the end was followed by another half acorn which when forced along the barrel by the plunger, with the butt pressed against the tummy, would surprise you by the loud bang forthcoming. Every bang and thunk were 'buties'. Many were the times when by sheer explosive force the barrel would split and one would have to resort to the ordnance depot (the shed) to forge a new barrel.

Being ever a boy at heart I have promised Sandra (my daughter) to produce one of these masterpieces before the acorns disappear, and we should have lots of fun, because little does he know it, but George is going to be pop-gunned around the gardens of Adam and Eve, and he's going to be very grumpy about it as well, I can tell you!

Regarding acorns, besides making great oaks, did you know that during the 1920s women and children of the village would gather them into bushel skeps (a wicker or osier basket with two woven handles) and sell them to farmers and pig keepers for fodder? I remember this being done; perhaps other readers could also bring it to mind; if you do, next time you see me, give me a wave!

[The following month Eva Pulford wrote in: 'Hello there, James, can you see me waving? I want to tell you about a sow that my husband once had. She could never be kept in and one day, just before farrowing, she escaped her pen and had her piglets halfway under a straw stack. All attempts at getting the young ones failed because the sow made herself very unpleasant to anyone who approached, so it was considered safest to leave them alone.

Quite soon they were old enough to come out and follow her about. It was autumn and she then, followed by five piglets, started a daily walk, which led between two rows of mangolds down to the bottom of the field. Then they climbed a bank into another field of roots, and down between two more rows of root crops. At length they came to an oak tree, and beneath it the acorns were large and plentiful. When they had eaten enough they returned the way they had come. The route never varied and in time they wore a track.

How did she become aware of an oak tree two fields away? I have always admired the independence and sagacity of that creature and her little band of nomads. Their trotters may have been sore, but their stomachs were full!]

The Cattle Yards

During the 1920s I always loved the month of September and indeed in later life I usually took some of my annual leave during this period. According to a person practising in astrology, seven is my lucky number and this beautiful month was the seventh in the Roman calendar. The hustle and bustle of haysel and harvest was ended and so was the extra money earned by the farmworkers. Of course 29th September is Michaelmas Day on which traditionally the farming year ended and land and buildings were offered for sale at auction.

Birds of all species would still be scratching and feeding on corn and various other seeds dropped amongst the stubble which as yet had not been ploughed in, and a wide selection of grubs, beetles and other insect life could be found. In the out-of-way corners and places, where rough ground was uncultivated and thistles flourished in abundance, I would watch the flocks of bullfinches, the handsome little fellows with deep red-breast plumage, black heads splashed with red and white patches, their wings also coloured with a splash of yellow. Their little cousins, the chaffinches, which throughout the countryside are more commonly known as 'draw-waters', would also be in community gatherings around the stacks of corn in the stackyard. They would be squabbling like old hens as they fought for possession of the brown and withering thistle stems now covered with a profusion of fluffy heads under the canopy of which the seeds would suffice for food whilst the supply lasted. Occasionally they would be startled and put to flight to flee from whatever it was that caused the alarm, perhaps a hovering hawk or a prowling mean and hungry-looking stray cat, and seeds would be scattered over a wide area causing much consternation to the land owner during the following season.

During the latter part of the month and into early October the mangolds and swedes would be harvested by cutting off the tops whilst still in the soil, and, using the same cutting hook, lifting them up and cutting off the small tap roots. Swedes were the valuable root crop used to feed cattle in the partly-covered cattle yards during the winter months. They were carted off the fields in horse-drawn 'tumblers' and stored in 'hales' alongside a field hedge near to the farm buildings, the hale being constructed by laying down a bed of straw and hedge trimmings, with the swedes being built up into a wedge-shaped mound stretching sometimes for fifty yards or more. The sides of the hale were covered with a thick layer of straw and then faced with a layer of earth which kept out the wet, frost and other ravages of winter months. Potatoes were, and in some places I believe are still, stored in the same way. Swedes are those elongated roots, ridged with leaf scars on the neck; they have purple skins with yellow/golden flesh and a top of bushy green leaves. They originally came to the British Isles from Sweden in the early 1800s, hence the name, and in consequence of large acreages grown in East Anglia for cattle feed, we took on the not-too-glamorous tag of 'Swede-bashers'. But the city and town folk who maligned us were not unpartial to enjoying them as a cooked vegetable.

However, far from the maddening crowds, there were many gaps to be seen along the rows across the fields, especially near the headlands, because when returning home from school during the afternoons, we were a hungry and ravenous lot and one would be 'borrowed'. We didn't need a knife to cut it up; a hefty throw on to the road surface would be sufficient to split it asunder and the succulent pieces would be devoured; the gustable essence still causes the 'slarvar to go barsark'.

However, from about the middle of September, cattle would be put into the partly-covered yards of the premises, bedded down with a plentiful supply of straw. Those to be fattened would be homebreds bought in from local farms and markets, some of which had spent the summer on the local marshes. I am told that about 90% would have been shipped over from Ireland.

I remember when my father was employed by Messrs William & Frank Molineux of Ashby Hall, immediately following harvest he would be working in the stackyard, busily engaged in thatching the corn stacks and when these had been wrapped up safe from the ravages of winter storms, gales and bitter winds, and the pernicious curiosity of 'them there blinkin owd crows and little owd sparrers', he would then apply his attentions to feeding the bullocks in the yards. Usually, cornstacks efficiently thatched stood the rigours of winter, especially so in a sheltered stackyard, but some not so well done and especially in outlying fields were ravaged by the winds and gales. One would often witness large holes in the thatch and watch as a crow, flying off with an ear of corn, the straw dangling, would be chased and molested by a screeching horde of 'sparrers'.

On some weekends and especially during school holidays, I would make myself available to assist my father and would cycle up to the farm where swedes and mangolds would be tipped up into the barn or turnip house and would be cut up in a root grinder, which was manufactured of cast iron and standing on four legs. Roots were thrown into the hopper and into contact with the cutting blades which, when rotated by turning a handle, would finish up like chips, these being deposited into a bushel 'skep' standing underneath. When the 'skep' was filled, the contents were dusted with chaff made from barley or oat straw and by the time my father had taken out one lot to the feed bins and returned, there was another one waiting to be taken out. Each bullock would eat approximately two bushels per day plus linseed oil cake and also upland hay fed to them from hayracks suspended above the feeder bins. The animals ate well, and being fed continuously it was a stark fact that the more they tucked away the fatter they became, which led to their eventual downfall when following a period of 10-12 weeks they would be placed on the market and sold for beef.

This was long before artificial fertilizers came into general use and every arable farmer counted among his capital equipment a yard full of bullocks, the purpose of which was also to supply and provide manure for future crops. Each day, or when necessary, straw would be placed in the yards to be compressed and compacted into a mass of solid manure which by the end of the season would be perhaps five or more feet high from ground level and locally referred to as 'lovely muck'. In this modern age it is apparent that costwise this method no longer exists and I was surprised when talking to Jonathan Molineux to find that he does still fatten some cattle by the old method, although he no longer turns the handle which operates the cutters on the grinder but has an engine to take the sting out of the grinding – so to speak. Nevertheless, I enjoyed my schooldays whilst helping my father in the bullock sheds, and on a cold winter's day the warmth and body heat from the cattle pervaded the inner buildings which were quite warm, and during the work we would stop and take a swig from a bottle of cold tea, no sugar or milk added, but just as it came from the pot.

About the end of March the yards would be cleared and muck-carting would ensue, using a horse and 'tumbler'. Heaps of eight to each load would be cromed off and set eight yards apart in line and rows. A crome was a thin tined fork with four tines turned over to an angle of 45 degrees and fitted with a long handle. Later, men would spread these heaps evenly over the land before ploughing commenced, and thus the old saying, 'From the land – to the land' was partly accomplished.

During the muck-carting and spreading there was always that pungent, penetrating rural aroma which weighed heavily on the atmosphere and which was very much loved and taken in by those people and visitors from the towns and cities as they passed through – somehow mocking those words by William Wordsworth in *Daffodils*: 'That floats on high o'er vales and hills', but perhaps they thought this was a mark of retaliation for daring to refer to us as 'Swede bashers'. Anyway I didn't mind, because after school I was out with my shovel and barrow collecting that which had inadvertently fallen from the loads, which in due course would assist our own vegetables to grow.

To us youngsters those heaps dotted over the fields meant nothing during daylight but in the early evening just after teatime when the mists came billowing and swirling in from over the marshes, enveloping the nearby fields, those heaps took on a more meaningful and sinister image. As their tops just emerged over the blanket of sea-like greyness, our fantasies

30

played tricks as we envisaged pigmy people living out there, or giant moles running berserk. Going to bed later on, the cupboards were searched and a good look under the bed was most essential to our safety before the candle was eventually blown out, following which any little noise or squeaky sound, or the loud wild shriek of a barn owl, would send our senses tingling. But the next morning all this was forgotten until the evening when once again that whitish grey canopy of nothingness came swirling and rolling over the marshes.

Regarding some parts of this story, I enlisted the help of a person who did at one time reside in Clippesby and was employed in the caring for and feeding of cattle but does not wish to be named. However, his daughter, Elizabeth, is employed at Fleggburgh Post Office and she will doubtless bring to mind to whom I refer without my divulging his name, and I haven't, have I? Of course I haven't, he specially requested me not to do so!

The Old-time Sugar Beet Harvest

You will all doubtless have noticed one of the main activities in the countryside at this time of year is that of harvesting sugar beet from the many farmlands. I have just had a week when I covered almost a thousand miles around East Anglia – Norfolk, Suffolk, Isle of Ely, Cambridgeshire and on to the borders of Huntingdonshire, and the tonnage of sugar beet piled high into enormous heaps, and those still in the fields, is almost unbelievable. But how simple it all seems, with a worker driving a tractor and pulling behind it a beet harvester which, as it moves over the rows of beet, cuts off the tops, lifts them from the soil and then gathers and hoists them on to a riddle, which during its upwards traverse shakes off most of the soil. The beet is then deposited from a chute into a receptacle being towed alongside by another tractor. In most cases the cut-off tops are shredded and left behind evenly spread in the wake of the machine, ready to be ploughed in. Once full, the towed receptacle is emptied onto a concrete foundation, where load after load is poured out, forming small hills. When a lorry arrives to be loaded, to transport the beet to the factory, again, how easy and simple it seems, with the use of a power hoist being filled by using a tractor bucket.

How different it is from that which I saw and knew during my younger days in the 1920s. I remember men during wet and freezing weather, wearing corn sacks slung over their shoulders and around their waists and knees to keep reasonably dry, digging up sugar beet one by one by using a small two-pronged fork, using one hand on the fork and the other grasping the beet top, pulling it clear of the soil, hitting the beet against the fork to remove sticky soil and then laying them in neat rows with all the tops pointing one way. When four or five rows had been pulled, the same ground was covered and, using a reaping type hook, but with two sharp pick-up prongs on the tip of the blade similar to a cheese knife, the worker would pierce the beet with the prongs, grasp it in one hand and with a quick blow cut off the leafy top, throwing the beet into small accumulating piles. Can you just imagine this being accomplished with every beet being individually lifted and then topped, having to be handled twice? When you next pass a large pile of sugar beet, just try to imagine how many hundreds of thousands there are, and try to visualize the arduous dedication with which the farm worker applied himself in bygone days. And you should have seen their hands! By handling wet beet all day long, huge cracks split the skin of the natural crevices between the joints of fingers and thumb, causing large swellings and bleeding, resulting in pain.

After the beet had been piled into heaps, along came a man with a horse and tumbril (tumbler) and the beet would be lifted up and thrown into this by using a specially designed fork. This fork had a usual-type shaft and handle grip but was larger and totally different from the normal fork in

32

that it had about six long, curved prongs set wide apart with blobs on the tine ends so as not to pierce the beet. The tines were set wide to allow any earth clods, stones and other debris to fall through. The tumbril was unloaded near a field gateway and the piles grew in size, looking exactly as they do today.

When the lorries came up to be loaded, this again was arduous, back-breaking work. It was all right whilst the loading space was only partly filled, as the beet only had to be thrown up, by the fork previously mentioned, a short distance in height, but to obtain a good heavy load, side and back rails were fitted to the lorry, and a fork full of beet would have to be thrown up some twelve to fifteen feet or more, and it took lots of throws and lots of forkfuls to fill up a large lorry.

Although we boys did sometimes help to load the beet on to the 'tumbler', we were never allowed to use a hook to cut the tops off; had this been so there would, without doubt, be quite a few of us with fingers and thumbs missing today. Whilst helping to load the lorry, we would on occasion throw a beet over the other side and then there would be a shout and words used which are now unprintable.

Whilst today the tops are discarded in most cases, they were once used as cattle-feed, and I well remember, as will quite a number of our readers, when they were fed to cows the result was that the milk tasted as if it had been laced with a mixture of castor oil and paraffin, and even the smell of it was most disagreeable.

When the lorries were overloaded it was inevitable whilst on their journey to the factory that large numbers of beet would fall off, as they rounded corners, and litter the roads, but these would become meal stores for the many creatures and wild fowl of the countryside. It would now be my Saturday morning chore to ride my bike around the roads and byways, picking up beet which had fallen, as these, when kept dry and allowed to get 'clung' after being cut into slices, would be an excellent supplement to winter fodder for our tame rabbits.

It was also most noticeable that lorry sizes increased, as did the tonnage they carried, resulting in the cutting of huge gaps into our road verges and banks. Most small villages within a radius of 10-15 miles supplied the workforce for Cantley factory, and all the men cycled to and from work during the sometimes bitter winter months. It seemed strange that such a valuable crop, grown to benefit the whole nation, had to be brought in during such inclement and wintry conditions. Very much like the fishermen who braved the seas to feed the nation with fish, these workers were sometimes scorned by the people of towns and cities as mindless clod-hoppers, but this was not so; they were men of strong will and character and body, and when I now see piles of beet and the beet harvester of today, I feel glad that times have changed, but reminiscent thoughts cannot be stifled.

This was also the era of the wherries, which plied their trade along our rivers, and Cantley factory, being on the river Yare, was supplied with large freights of beet. As a boy I would gaze across the marshes to see the massive black sail which embraced the wintry wind to propel such a large craft through the water.

The Bramble Blackberry

A great affinity has always existed between country folk and that luscious black fruit of the hedgerows and commons, probably because it was the most easily obtainable – but not always so easily accessible – and of course for free, and none more so than in our own rural haunts and by-ways of Norfolk villages.

As a small boy I remember the hedgerows being full of God-provided fruits, and during the weekends in the afternoons and early evenings the whole family would be out with bowls, baskets, basins and dishes taking advantage of the economic potential of blackberries. The children of course would be eating as many as were placed into the given receptacles (and I was no exception) and with their arms and legs scratched and lacerated by the cruel bramble barbs, as if nature was loath and unwilling to yield up her wealth too easily without a struggle – the tell-tale purple-stained mouths and faces mingled well with the runny noses of the younger ones. But the mothers would calmly retort, 'That'll do him – or har – a world of good, better than a good dollop of syrup of figs'.

As is always the situation, the biggest and juiciest fruits were always out of arms' reach, but our mothers and grannies were not to be outdone as each carried a crook stick to reach up and grip the bramble head and haul down the fruit to submission. These crook sticks were cut and were also the produce of the hedgerows and out of season were seen suspended from a nail driven into the wall of the family shed keeping close company with the onions and shallots until brought down for the next season's gathering.

Having filled one basket, this would be placed on the ground whilst another was being filled, and although it was a foolish act to do this, and calamity occurred every so often, it was done without aforethought and I well remember getting one of my first 'dings of the lug' for inadvertently kicking over a basket and spilling the contents.

Later on at home I remember the fervour of jam and jelly preserving, the boiling pot bubbling away like a witch's cauldron, and after the sugar and lemon juice had been added, emitting that pungent tangy aroma which pervaded the entire household until the set had been obtained. In some cases this was frustration in its element when blob after blob of juice came into contact with a cold saucer and the tell-tale smear and wrinkling was not forthcoming. The sweet fragrance was bound to attract the unwelcome attention and hindrance of the 'yellow and black critters', the wasps, but these were either swatted away or directed against that odious sticky strip of gummy fly paper hanging suspended from the ceiling – most efficient in their day but terribly messy things, were they not?

Afterwards, filling, or perhaps adorning would be a more appropriate description, the shelves of the walk-in pantry, would be jars containing jams and jellies, all of which were pure goodness of nature, some embellished with other fruits, to be relished after summer had faded into autumn and the winter reared its unfriendly and menacing features.

During these winter months a pleasant touch of summer would reappear when the jam was put to many good uses, those numerous and varied tarts, puddings and pies covered with creamy custard. Especially I remember that buttered crust of home-made bread with loads of jam thickly spread thereon being demolished on returning home from school. These pleasures more than compensated for the 'Ding of the lug', scratched and punctured skin and the squeezing and probing for those irritating thorns which had embedded themselves into fingers and hands.

How scrumptious those toasted home-made scones were, covered with blackberry jelly, eaten and tucked into whilst sitting cross-legged in front of a roaring fire, whilst outside the snow lay cold and deep, resentful of the fact we were still tasting the pleasures of summer gone. Whilst the frost engraved its many and wonderful varied patterns on the window panes, they seemed to brighten up the inclement weather, and again as one remembered the scratches and the sore fingers and thumbs from those protecting brambles ... who cared?

It was also very surprising what other uses were found for this free gift of the summer days. During the long winter months when the sniffles, coughs and sneezes were looked upon as normal and seasonable, yet were outrageous, contagious and continuous, it was comforting, before being packed off to bed, to sip a small glass of blackberry jelly to which had been added a small quantity of boiling water to concoct one of nature's healing syrups. And what's more, as mother used to say, 'It'll do you a lot more good than that there shilly shally old stuff what Doctor Roydon puts into them there bottles of his'.

But beware, there is always something abounding which tends to spoil the enjoyment of each and everyone of us in our pleasures. Did you know that superstitious folklore has it that on Michaelmas Day the devil puts his feet on all the blackberries which are left ungathered and it is considered extremely unlucky to eat them after 29th September of each year, and I would take a guess quite considerably unhealthy too, for after all, you never know where his feet may have been! However, I am not in the least worried about him and his tantrums; my jars of blackberry jelly are looking exceptionally resplendent and colourful on my shelves and fortunately I do not have to resort to the roadside hedgerows, most of which are now tainted with various sprays, pesticides and diesel fumes; no, to the contrary, although I reside in the city of Norwich, I am fortunate in having a large garden and at the rear down one side of the boundary fence this is devoted to a whole stretch of blackberry bramble of the wild variety. Thorns, yes – I still get them embedded in my fingers and hands and usually have to suffer with a certain amount of patience until I visit Sandra at Clippesby, who as they say in Norfolk parlance 'prooges them out for me'. I also have the thornless species but this is not used for jams and preserves but favoured more as a dessert.

I suppose my front garden is not one of the tidiest along Dereham Road, but it is a fair size and people will stop and look and gesture, which of course is their prerogative and sometimes, if it is two inquisitive ladies who can still visualize it in its Victorian splendour, I sometimes wander outside, and being ladies they ask outright, 'Do you like your garden untidy like that?' Not taken aback in any way I blithely answer that it is a conversational garden and it has achieved exactly that situation for them, but, I explain, it is also a conservational garden as well, because at the rear of the house it is more than a wee bit wilder than the front.

It is large and I have moles and voles, mice and the occasional rat, spiders, stag beetles and ants, every creepy thing you can imagine, the sometimes unwanted snake, hedgehogs, numerous birds which pinch my fruit and all the cats from homes which do not possess a garden. I have a wonderful display of white flowers which other people destroy because they don't like bindweed and I foster several clumps of stinging nettles to encourage butterflies and moths. They smile courageously and I mention the wild brambles and the blackberries which are an uncontrolled mess but when I tell of the uninvited, unwanted guest after 29th September they really do look concerned and it's amusing to see them scuttle away on their walking sticks at the double, casting sudden and furtive looks over their shoulders wondering perhaps if they ought to inform the appropriate institution or not and it's most amusing whilst shopping at the Co-op, also on the Dereham Road, the queer looks I receive and the heads nodding in my direction.

But however, and nevertheless, after the 29th September when the leaves are gently rustling as if in whispered conversation, of course I am most conscious of the brambles tittering away to each other and maybe some day if I am stealthy enough in my approach I will probably hear – 'watch out......there's a D...... about'.

I know it's like teaching Grannie to tie her bonnet strings but I'll risk it...the next time you make blackberry jelly, when you add the sugar to the juice, also include just a level teaspoonful of mixed spice to each pound of sugar and later taste what a special difference this makes.

What! you already know about this ...sorry I mentioned it.

Winter on the Marshes

In the 1920s during winter afternoons when snow was with us, I would often walk across the marshes where I could wander aimlessly and at will, treading the frosted tufts of grass now powdered with fallen snowflakes. Gone were the cattle and most wildlife, and the insects which abounded in profusion during the summer were now in hiding. I might on occasions have disturbed a hare which would lollop away and in its course upset a party of golden plovers, which at the sudden interruption would squeal in dismay at being disturbed.

The wild flowers which blossomed in untamed profusion during the summer had long since withered and now the spindly stalks were encrusted with ice, the seed vessels that were left glistening with icy diamonds that resembled miniature chandeliers sparkling in the fading light. The grasses and reeds on the dyke's waterline, once green, vibrant and beautiful were now bedraggled, the stems bent and the reed tops broken, their mops curled into crystal plumes, shimmering, as a soft breeze breathed over and along the dyke. The once proud yellow flag iris were now forlorn, their arrogance smitten with the icy blast of the cold winter winds. The green speckled duckweed which blanketed the dykes during the summer was now beset like congealed green salad, forming a contrast with the tall brown stems of once proud grasses now huddled closely together as if to afford support to each other in an effort to sustain life and existence.

Where nature, overnight, had transformed the countryside into a fairy grotto, even the little black waterhens with their twitching white tails had forsaken their favourite marshlands and now frequented the more habitable ditches and waterways in plantations and woods; though one could still define the footprints and padmarks of some more hardy animals and birds, and most certainly the little black velvet-coated gentleman, often maligned for spoiling lawns and grassland, was very much alive and hunting laboriously for a meal. The usually hard-working windmills were silent, their giant sails motionless and still, the hulks of their framework not unlike giant statues, cold and naked.

Alone, I could slither and slip in a dreamland of nature's wonderful fantasies; I saw the frozen webs of spiders between the long stems of thistles and docks, sparkling as if they had been dusted by the hand of a supernatural being; the insects which had supplied the spiders' needs were now just glinting multi-shapen icy spheres.

Although cold, I was mostly oblivious to it, and as the watery old sun hung his head over towards 'Will's Mother's' and before the dusk enveloped and blotted out the landscape and I became frightened of the often-mentioned marsh spooks and hikey-sprites, I heard heartening calls from the gradually darkening sky, and looking up, saw wild geese in perfect 'V' formation flying at several hundred feet, the leader sounding his 'follow me' call note. Skein after skein passed above me and again I thought on the wonders of nature. I could not hear the swish of feathered wing beats, only the call of the leaders as they kept in touch with each formation, but what a majestic sight! I watched as in the distance they swooped gracefully down onto the Acle, Stokesby and Fleggburgh marshes for a well-deserved feed of marsh grass.

Not long afterwards I heard the loud reports of shotguns and the calls of terror as these lovely birds rose again into the sky to find fresh pastures. I wondered why this should be so – they were not akin to rabbits and rats, who bespoil and damage crops and food, and were deservedly looked upon as vermin – but creatures of innocent habits, graceful and dignified in flight.

Although a young mischievous rascal, I had a natural love of the wild and my heart bled for my feathered friends, and on arriving home my mother noticed I had been crying. Going to bed, I tormented myself with the thought that these geese had perhaps travelled thousands of miles from as far as North Scandinavia, Russia and the Arctic tundra, having suffered more hardships than the average human has to contend with, only to be shot at and maimed on our own local marshes. Hot tears would sting my eyes before I said my prayers and dropped off to sleep, the troubled thoughts burdening my heart gradually slipping into the distance.

The next morning as I went off to school, I would listen to our well-adjusted clock – the train – rumbling across the long bridge spanning Breydon Water, and start thinking about the essay I would write, embracing my weekend, receiving encouraging remarks from the headmaster; but not long after I would be holding out my outstretched palm once again to receive the punishing cane for some silly misdeed or other.

P. S. Whilst during the spring and summer months our little feathered friends 'pinch and nick' our soft fruits, block our gutterings with nesting materials, and splash our windows, they also provide us with amusement with their varied antics; and who could possibly adorn themselves in the fine feathers they fashion themselves with? During the winter's cold, please don't forget to feed the little 'perishers' to nourish and help keep them alive and chirpy!

When the Broads Froze

During one long winter in the 1920s I remember there was a heavy fall of snow following which a prolonged hard frost set in and lasted for several weeks. The water in all the 'deeks' surrounding the many separate holdings on the marshes and elsewhere were frozen over. Wildlife searched for water and this was mostly supplied for their comforts by the aptitude of the ever-diligent marshman who would break the ice over a fairly wide area thus allowing animals to drink and the wildfowl and birds not only to drink but to have a daily bathe. It is not always well known that birds need a bathe frequently, and after preening their feathers are well suited for a night in cold weather; a clean 'ole badd' is a warm 'ole badd' when the feathers are fluffed out.

I could never skate, but there were one or two in the villages who could, and off the nail in the shed came the skates, the blades of which had been well oiled and wrapped in cloth or sacking to fend off the rust and taken down occasionally for a check, awaiting the right time.

Commencing from the 'longspring' at Billockby corner one could skate to the windmill at Stokesby turning, along the roadside 'deek' to the Muckfleet and along the intersecting ways to Burgh common finishing again at the starting place. A long distance in a very short time, much faster than a cycle could be ridden.

One excellent skater stands out in my memory, Herbert 'Harbart' Hunn, the husband of Susy and father of Margaret, Billy and Reggie with all of whom I went to school. He acquired a most unusual nickname of 'Aerioh' and why, I do not know. Although nicknames were commonplace and easy to associate with the person, this one always escaped me and it is much too late to find the answer now. At the time they lived in the far end of a row of houses, those still standing and on which the cement facing can be seen on the right hand foreground when approaching the village from Acle river bridge. The road end house is still occupied by Joyce Curtis, one of the well-known benefactors to the village and a long time resident.

Those of us who could not skate (we couldn't afford to buy the skates for one thing) would cause a long slide to be made along the centre of the road which, much to our enjoyment, was the next best thing. We would have slides of up to twenty and twenty-five feet in length and a short run to reach the slide would see us with one foot in front of the other, arms outstretched to keep a good balance and there we were enjoying a cold and rigorous winter. The slide continued until along cometh that once long-ago and well-known road lengthman, 'Prushia' from Fleggburgh who, midst a barrage of snowballs, would set about the destruction of our slide with shovel after shovel of gritting material. Gone was the polished glassy surface, but as soon as his back was turned and he was less than a quarter mile along the road we had established another one.

Also at this time, I think it must have been December 1925 – January 1926, according to records, the mild weather which set in at Christmas 1925, continued until January 12th 1926, when it gave place to nine days of a severity unparalleled except in our coldest winters. On the night of the 15th the thermometer on the ground fell to minus 10.2 degrees recording the lowest temperatures since 9th February 1919. The next day, following a phenomenon of nature, the word went round the villages like wildfire, 'the Broads have frozen over,' and indeed so they had. Such was the intensity of the freeze there was no need to go through the age-old saying we all at sometime chanted, 'Bends she breaks, cracks she bear'; Jack Frost in his element had created a fairyland playground. I well remember what great fun everyone had from the young to the oldest, and people walked for miles around converging on the group of Broads. We, from Clippesby and also Billockby, walked there and back, this was the time when I did not yet own a boneshaker bike. There was skating, sledging and dancing and even fire

41

braziers on sleds to beat off the cold, in addition to which roast chestnuts and potatoes were enjoyed. When I speak of this to our younger generation they look at me askance and question that this actually happened but I can assure all our readers this did take place, and there are still senior citizens in the area who can vouch for the authenticity of the event.

Whilst this weather persisted, heavy curtains were taken from the linen cupboards and tin trunks to cover windows and doors to keep out the biting cold.

Looking out from my bedroom window I viewed the white wilderness of the marshes that took on a forlorn look of sadness, bereft or so it seemed of all living creatures and just biding time, waiting for the moment when in God's good time spring approached, and when first the strips and tussocks of reeds would appear and later, once again, the lush green grass, transforming the landscape to its more familiar and pleasant aspect. The search would begin again along the banks and bottoms of hedgerows for the first sight of the weak but encouraging snowdrops and primroses, the little flowers that would herald the not-so-far-off spring. These were proudly presented to the school teacher, and later because of some misdemeanour when a 'Ding of the lug' was forthcoming it was hoped that the 'ding' would be much less in substance. I would watch as an old 'harnser' passed overhead and within sight, seeming weary in his heavy-laboured flight. His meals were now almost non-existent, and no longer could he summon up strength to sound his 'kronk' call that all was well.

During the 1947 deep freeze, I watched this on the Pathé News Reel from the more sunny climes of Cairo and Beirut, and I thought of my boyhood days, having the river and marshes on one side, the sea on the other, with the Broads in between, remembering those far-off days midst old-time surroundings now vanished into obscurity, never to return.

They have ever been to me a constant source of pleasure and especially so during my years of military service in Europe and the Middle East when I was able to turn tragic times into fair days, remembering and recalling all the old haunts, and revelling in the nostalgic mists of time.

I wished I could have been in Alexandria, Port Said, Suez or Damascus when during the following extra-cold phase in 1963-64 a prolonged spell of deep frost lasted for about three months.

Again, along the waterways of our countryside, a great loss of wildlife and waterfowl was counted, among which were large numbers of that long-legged and scraggy old scamp, the scourge of garden ponds and small fisheries alike - that eagle-eyed old scoundrel, the 'Harnser.'

Nature's Weather Forecasts

Although very much scoffed at and the source of derision, there is a wealth of weather lore which has been accumulated by close observation of those who have spent their lives in the country. According to this, although our climatic conditions are fickle, nature in itself provides a variety of weather pointers in the activities of plants and animals, together with certain conditions of the land and water, and in our part of East Anglia referred to by the unwise as 'living in the sticks', in particular, the sky.

Although our skies contain many clues to the weather of the ensuing hours, soft and delicate clouds are an indication of fair and fine weather, but heavy cloud formations generally lead to deterioration. There is no need for anyone to be told that when in the distance a rumble of thunder is heard and the clouds, as it is said in Norfolk, as 'black as yar hat', there would be no need to wonder but to get as quickly as possible under the nearest cover, because, 'there's a rare old gooden comin up'.

Big fleecy cumulus clouds sailing merrily through the sky at about seven or eight in the morning usually melt away by ten and unrelieved sunshine follows. When a cloud forms together instead of drifting openly then it can easily build up into a storm. The colours of the sky, too, have their weather meanings and portents. For instance the red sky at night is said to be the shepherd's delight. It is more likely to be if the red is not too bright and lurid. A bright yellow sky denotes wind. A pale yellow sky more often than not brings rain while an orange or copper-coloured sky usually results in both wind and rain.

43

A red or gaudy sunrise signifies bad weather by mid-day. A purple or black dawn on the other hand is reckoned to be a good sign for a reasonable day. Greenish tints in the sky are there only momentarily and only occur during periods of unsettled weather; they are purported to be a reliable warning that rain is imminent.

Dew on the grass in the morning is usually a sign of a fine day to follow and an old couplet tells us,

> *'The dews of the evening industriously shun,*
> *they're the tears of the sky for the loss of the sun.'*

The moon also plays its part in foretelling the weather with the following advice.

> *'If the moon shines like a silver shield, be not afraid to reap your field,*
> *but if she rises haloed round, soon we'll tread on deluged ground.'*

I often heard my brother Freddie quote the old saying, 'There's a burrer round the moon tonight; I don't like the look of that.'

Many animals and insects are sometimes sensitive to approaching stormy weather. The spider is a particularly good weather forecaster and prophet. It will adjust the anchor lines of its web at least every twenty-four hours in order to counteract any weather changes and usually seems to have quite a few hours' warning of impending wind and rain. Long anchor threads are a sign of continued fine weather but the threads are shortened as the prospect of deterioration arises. Spiders stop work in the rain but if they do continue it is a sure and certain sign of it being only a quick short shower or they are extremely famished. Clever little devils, aren't they? I know they do not like water because many has been the time when I have rescued one from my water butt and was thanked most graciously with a flash from vivid red eyes and the flapping of beautiful long eye lashes!

Both domestic and wild duck are extremely sensitive to sudden changes of air pressure. This is because they have very thin skulls which warn them of an approaching storm and make them restless. The domestic fowl can be literally a weather cock (excuse the pun), and if a cock crows when he goes to bed he often wakes to a wet morning. A longer term prediction is provided by the old country saying,

*'If the cock moult before the hen, we shall have weather thick and thin,
but if the hen moults before the cock, we shall have weather hard as a rock.'*

So there you are Janet, 'just watch them there ole chickens of yours,'
and Richard Fox, 'just keep a weather eye on them there ducks.'

Signs of rain are provided by many creatures. A watery portent is when
glow-worms shine bright and are seen more often; also when snails cross
roads and paths. A once commonly-known saying was that when cows lie
down there is going to be rain. More accurate perhaps is the following,

*'When a cow tries to scratch her ear, it means a shower is very near.
When it thumps its ribs with its tail, look out for thunder, lightning and hail.'*

Moles often work industriously near the surface just before a cold spell.
Pigs become very lively when a strong wind is coming – they are said to be
able to smell the wind and they usually retreat to their sty well before the
storm reaches them.

Plants too offer some fairly reliable tips as to the future weather pattern. Chickweed, daisies and dandelions all close their petals when it is going to be wet and stormy. The scarlet pimpernel is not named the poor man's weather glass without good reason. The leaves of maple, sycamore, lime, plane and poplar tremble and show their undersides before a storm. A further long-term forecast comes from,

'If the oak is out before the ash, you should only get a splash.
If the ash is out before the oak, you will surely get a soak.'

Many villagers who live near a pond will testify to the truth of this old couplet,

'When ditch and pond offend the nose,
then look for rain and strong blows.'

Interpreting the varying weather signs of local flora and fauna has been going on in and around villages for centuries. Maybe there are not so many who believe the old jingles these days but one thing is certain, they are more pleasing and sound much better than the meteorological (coo that's a hard one) statistics concerning 'troughs of low pressure' and 'deep depressions.' Neither can it be denied that in any immediate locality nature's weather forecasters can be more accurate than all the highly-expensive gadgetry at a distant weather station.

My grandfather used to say, 'Them there old rooks and crows are kiken up a lotta shindy tonite, cawren and a halleren. I'm gorn to rack up my rabbits arly'. He knew this was a sign of bad weather.

I can also tell you one thing for sure; it is no earthly good going fishing when an east wind is blowing, 'you ount git nuthen batta than a cronic corf an a bad chist.' So there!

AT HOME

Clippesby Cottages

The 1920s Wash Day

If there is one thing which stands out more clearly than anything else during the 1920s, it is the drudgery of family washday, always on a Monday. I well remember how my mother slaved away at it, from dawn to dusk. If only I could have wished on her one of the plumbed-in, computerised, programmed, beautiful luxuries we have today, with the various warm and hot washes, several rinses and the systematic controlled spin-drying, following which the whole load is transferred to a tumble dryer to leave it ready for ironing! With the latest types of steam irons and ironing boards this is sheer luxury, 'Says he'! A small family business only a stone's throw from me in Norwich City has come up with a novel idea of 'You wash, we iron,' and exactly as they point out, the modern washing machine and tumble dryer do the hard bits and as one goes to work, so the wash is left and collected after work already neatly pressed and ironed.

How totally different it was when I was a youngster! Every household had one – that is, a copper, either in the scullery, kitchen or outside shed. Ours was in the scullery, or back place, as we used to call it, fixed in a brick surround with a fire grate underneath for the coals or wood, covered with a round wooden lid top with a lifting handle. Standing beside this in the corner, highly painted in red or green, sometimes a variation of both, in view to all callers to the back door, was the most essential darling of washday blues – the mangle – and leaning against this, the schoolboy's nightmare, to wit – the copper stick.

Preparation began by filling the copper with about four to six buckets of water, either from the well or a clacker pump which nine times out of ten had to be primed before any water was forthcoming, or if the soft water butts collecting rainwater from the house roof were full, water from these would be used. I would content myself by doing this the evening before, after church, and it took me an appreciable amount of time, as at this time I could only manage to handle a half bucket full.

I am still of the opinion that the reason why so many people attended church on Sunday in those days was to pray and beseech the good Lord to send favourable weather with a good breeze on the morrow!

However, notwithstanding the elements, I would be up early and, placing paper within the fire grate and finely chopped kindling on top, would light up, and after igniting would place coals on top, and once a

good fire had resulted would then keep this constant with a good stoke up of my very own sawn and chopped-up-to-correct-size wood.

Automatic washing powder, Persil, Bold, Ariel, Daz – you name it, we didn't have any! Our commodities were simple, and there was nothing to compare with either a solid long bar of 'Sunlight' or 'Watson's' soap. (Coo! I'll bet some of the great-grannies are enjoying this!) As the water got hot, slices of soap were placed in with the clothes, and once the boil was reached the copper stick was used to move them around.

Another essential item was the scrubbing brush; some of my linen certainly needed its gentle caress. After a good boiling, again using the copper stick, all the linen was transferred to a large galvanised bath where any stubborn marks were dissolved with the use of a contraption made from a wooden frame and overlapping wood slats, using plenty of soap and elbow grease, a wash board, which blossomed to far-reaching fame during the 1950s when they produced a distinctive rattle in the 'Skiffle' groups.

After several rinses, in comes the ancient spin dryer – the afore-mentioned mangle, a heavy cast-iron implement of four iron wheels, two round, long wooden rollers adjusted for tension by a clumsy wheel/handle situated at the top, which when turned applied pressure to a series of steel springs and thence to the rollers. Cast-iron cogs attached to the rollers and likewise to a large iron wheel turned by a wooden handle would engage the whole works. Woe betide anyone whose fingers were caught up in the washing! A wooden trough took the expelled water from the squeezed linen into a receptacle, and another board directed the linen to fall into a basket!

Most houses had fairly large gardens and alongside the pathways were strong, tall posts to which were attached wire lines. These had to be carefully wiped before hanging the linen out. The prop (promp) was a long wooden pole with a 'Y' at the top end to engage the line and hoist the linen up into the wind. It was a common occurrence that no matter how sturdy the posts in the ground, or how taut the line, the weight of the linen always sagged, enforcing the consequent use of the 'promp'.

As a matter of interest, I still own an old mangle, with which I am quite pleased, probably manufactured at the turn of the century, but alas the wooden rollers are in sad repair. It looks quite ancient, which in fact it is, but catches the eye with its wrought iron decorations. Quite readable is the inscription 'JOHNSON – BURTON – THEOBALD – NORWICH – M V 24 – SUPERB REGISTERED'.

However, there is now the ironing to do, and mind you there is no fancy-shaped ironing board or beautiful lightweight steam iron; the kitchen table would suffice and the irons were of heavy cast iron, one on the fire and one being used. There was a piece of cloth in the hearth to wipe them as they came off the fire. Once finished, the linen was stacked away and folded in drawers and cupboards upstairs, sprinkled with a generous supply of lavender sachets. How lovely these smelt!

Had it been a wet day it would have been a different story entirely, as clothes would then be strung across the ceilings attached to wires stretching from corner to corner. There was no other way, and every time one moved one would get a wet slap from a shirt tail or a dangling sleeve. George was telling me that in the City whilst living in a 'two-up, two-down' with no garden, this was a weekly occurrence and everyone just took it as another part of living.

Electricity didn't find its way to us until about 1936/7, when at least the electric boiler 'het' the water and removed one difficulty of fire-lighting and stoking. It wasn't until about 1947, I think, that Lucy and I were on army leave, and in Great Yarmouth we espied a new-fangled electric washer which heated the water and had a rotor blade, but one which had a handle fixed and still had to be motivated manually. This was the latest model and my mother was overjoyed at owning one – it was of immense help to her. We named it our 'Wishy washy piddle paddle machine', as that is how it sounded as the rotor splashed round.

The Wall Oven

Often when I am not either driving or dashing around here and there I find it most pleasant to sit by the fire during the evening to reminisce and meditate, when inevitably my thoughts deviate to those distant and far-off days of the 1920s and my boyhood.

I always settle down to dinner about 6.30–7.00 pm and, after preparation, this is cooked by modern conveniences such as a gas oven and grill, supplemented by a microwave and sometimes a pressure cooker. An electric coffee percolator or jug kettle quickly and efficiently dispenses the beverage of my choice, or I resort to the refrigerator for a cool beer or fruit drink. Later on if I fancy toast or cheese on toast, this is most efficiently brought to plate by using an electric toaster, modern grill or sandwich maker. Then, whilst sipping my brandy, I think of those days long ago when none of us in the country villages had any such luxuries. I remember well the cooking facilities with which my own family survived.

Firstly there was the fire in the living room with the cast-iron grate and slightly raised hob, on either side of which the large iron kettle rested, simmering quietly and waiting patiently to be brought quickly to boiling point for that ever-refreshing cup of tea. An iron fender surrounded the stove to assist in arresting any falling coals or wood, and inside this stood the heavy iron pots of up to 10 pint capacity which were brought into use to boil the vegetables and also quite large enough to hold those delicious dumplings and 'Norfolk Swimmers' which were floated on top of the 'tearters'. If a kettle and saucepan were already on the hobs and other utensils were also needed for additional purposes, then an appendage was brought into use which fitted onto bars in front of the grate.

The wall oven – ours was situated in what we termed to be the back kitchen or scullery – was a remarkable contrivance which sufficed for baking bread, pies, tarts, buns and puddings, also meats, when the poultry or joints and toad-in-the-hole and Yorkshire puddings sizzled away merrily. The oven itself was constructed of mild steel, flat at the bottom, with an oval top, just one inner shelf in the middle, the door being fitted with a brass door knob which when pulled and pushed, cleared and removed excessive accumulated soot from the top of the oven. Need I tell you that these brass door knobs were always highly polished? To supply the heat, a long narrow grate was situated underneath to hold the coals or wood, and the most remarkable situation regarding these ovens was the fact that there were no dials or instruments, nor thermostatic adjustments, to gauge the progressive or diminishing heat to ascertain that precise amount for each baking.

Today, bread has to be baked for a specified time at a constant heat to achieve the perfect loaf, and similarly for cakes and pastries; but our grannies and mothers had no knobs and dials to twist and turn to moderate or give excess heat, but relied entirely on their own capabilities and judgement, and I know that all the lovely foods baked and cooked in our oven were absolutely perfect. There was nothing more tasty than a nice hot roll or the crust of a loaf smothered with farm butter and folded over a wedge of cheese.

Naturally, I had to assist with the running of our household and amongst my many chores were to chop kindling wood, fetch in the coal and wood and lay and light the fires. Drawing water from the well was the most difficult for me as a full pail of water was very heavy, but I easily got around this by only filling half the bucket from the well and transferring this to another bucket standing on a bench outside the back door. I did not mind at all having to lay and light the fires, as by doing so I always had the first chance of a good warm, and furthermore, being the chief stoker for my mother, especially at the oven grate, I also had the chance to prepare vegetables, and later progressed to the stage of baking and making pastry.

Eventually whilst still quite young I could prepare and cook the meals for my family whilst my mother was able to attend to other work. I felt most pleased with myself when at about the age of 11-12 years I prepared and cooked our Christmas dinner, but had to call for help to lift the turkey out of the oven in order to baste it, and I will admit here and now, my sausage rolls were scrumptious. As for the jam tarts – well, they were out of this world! My grandfather often remarked to my father, 'There's one thing sartin, Will, that there boy might be a rare little warmin, but he can sartanly tann out them there wittles suffen good.'

I must also mention that in accordance with other households we had a refrigerator – well, of a kind – this being a wooden structure, a sort of framed box, the outside of which was covered with a fine wire mesh to keep out the 'unwanteds', and this was secured to the outside wall of the house and always fixed in the coldest position possible. It served reasonably well. During summer a string bag containing commodities such as butter, milk and other perishables were dropped down the well on a piece of rope to a depth where it was nice and cool, and this primitive method did actually keep foods from going off, if only for a short period.

To make toast, one had to possess a long three-pronged toasting fork and hold the bread before a coal fire. I know it is still done in this way more or less as a gimmick, but when I was a youngster if I wanted toast this was the only way to get it.

What a bind it was to fill the portable paraffin lamp each night, to clean the glass funnel and trim the wick when necessary! But when lit there was a very pleasant glow to compensate for the inconvenience. Later on paraffin-oil-powered ovens came into fashion and these were quite efficient, but there were always those overpowering fumes within the house which tended to sting the eyes. When these were in general use, a hawker would travel around the villages with a horse and cart on which was fixed a large capacity tank filled with paraffin, and in keeping with other vendors and tradesmen, he would call out his commodity and use a handbell to advertise his whereabouts. If perchance anyone in Clippesby or Billockby did run out of this evil-smelling liquid, this was also obtainable in small quantities from Hudson's shop, the wooden shop with a thatched roof, but the only setback against this was that after serving a customer with oil, the next customer would probably – and did – receive butter, sugar or cheese slightly tainted! Shopkeepers in the country in my days were not so fussy as they have to be today, and it was either 'Take it or leave it' – or walk the two miles to Acle or Fleggburgh – and this meant you took it.

What a godsend it was when electricity first arrived in the villages, around 1937! But again even this was fraught with its frustrations, as the meter had a hungry appetite and, being fed with shillings, there was always a clamour to obtain these coins and, having no gauge to tell how much of a shilling's worth of electricity was left, if anyone was not careful enough it meant sudden darkness and back to the candle and oil lamp. Then came the trudge from door to door – 'Hev ya gotta spare shillin?' It also became a recognised request when anyone went shopping: 'Would you put a shilling in the change, please?'

With electricity came the electric oven and kettle 'in hot pursuit'; both were a godsend and for some unknown reason when our first and original kettle packed in working, it was placed away in a cupboard and forgotten about. I have it today – the copper kettle – which served my family for a brew of tea in the mornings, during the day, and for the nightly cup of cocoa before retiring to bed. With its heavy element it was nearly as weighty as the old iron kettle used on the hob, but obviously much more convenient and, unlike modern kettles and jugs with fast boiling elements, was very much slower in coming to the boil.

Coming out of my reverie I think to myself – what a laugh it all was! – and topping my glass up with a last brandy – I pop off up the wooden hill to bed and more often than not I dream of the good old days – so some say! But I have a feeling deep down that I prefer the present, with all its luxuries, even if it does have its alarming situations.

The Well in our Garden

Perhaps it would be presumptuous of me to ask if anyone has ever been in the situation where, whilst doing something, some action, either physical or vocal, immediately prompts the mind to deviate from its intended point, and leaves it stranded from its original objective?

I suppose I could place the blame for my lapses on being in the autumn of my life now, and prone to nostalgic memories, and re-iterate the words of John Keats when he said about autumn, 'Season of mists and mellow fruitfulness', remembering its sorrows and joys alike.

But, to make my point, on one such occasion recently when with the 'Repps Revellers' giving a concert at Upton and reciting that humorous piece about 'Albert and the Lion', I had only got as far as, 'A grand little lad was young Albert, all dressed in his best, what a swell, and a stick with an 'orses 'ead 'andle, the finest that Woolworths could sell,' when, 'Splot!' – I went back in time momentarily, savouring and recalling those days during the late 1920s when I went to Woolworth's in Great Yarmouth and bought my first magnet.

A number of people will doubtless remember still and visualise the store where the selling power was enhanced with the gimmick of 'Nothing over 6d' – and one could purchase almost everything, from a packet of pins to a tin kettle, a doll or toy, a lipstick or rouge.

As I pointed out, I bought my first magnet at Woolworth's, and reading the instructions, revelled in the fact it could retrieve almost everything which had been placed in hidden crevices and out-of-the-way places and even in water.

Getting back home I couldn't wait to try out my magnet, and where better to test its great possibilities than to drop some nails and metal objects down the well? It did its job fine and I revelled in the powers of my new-found object of enjoyment.

Next door, Aunt Beatie Prime was washing up and came out to ascertain 'what the little old boy was up to' and was so much taken aback with my new-found power that she with every confidence and without thinking threw some of her best knives and forks down the well. Naturally and with a smug grin on 'young Jimma's fearse' the magnet was lowered, and sweeping the bottom of the well seemed to ignore the cutlery but did come up with one of my large nails. I began to wonder, and my 'little od hart was a-goin ten to the dozen' but nevertheless dropped my marvellous magnet into the well again making a sweep, but came up with nothing. I looked at Beatie and quickly she put two and two together, and with a 'You young -----!' (I dare not put into words what she said) swung her hand with the intended 'ding of the lug'. I just managed to duck as she swung her hand, and as her hand swished over my head, causing much wind, I was off like a shot.

And – do you remember, Beatie? – because you couldn't catch me I taunted you and stuck out my tongue and pulled a face, more in thankfulness for not being caught than anything else, and you, pointing your finger at me, remarked, 'Mind there isn't a sudden bolt of lightning and you are stuck like that!' Do you know, I sometimes wonder about that remark, but I cannot remember the bolt of lightning.

It wasn't until later I found out that stainless steel objects and other like alloys were beyond the capabilities of my poor little 'ha-penny' magnet. 'How-sum-avar', as they say in Norfolk, we all have the right to be wrong now and then, but it seemed as if I was wrong most of the time.

I like to brighten up someone's day, so if during the first few days of January, 1991, you see Beatie walking around Fleggburgh with a smile on her face you will know why, and if perchance she's been in the Village Hall playing bingo it won't be because she's just won a prize, but simply because the mists of time have rolled away for a brief moment in her long life, and once again she sees her knives and forks shimmering and shining up from the bottom of the well, and she hasn't an earthly hope of catching me when running at full pelt along our garden path.

In the meantime, there I was in front of fifty or more people at Upton, and couldn't think of the next line, but laughingly focussed on one lady and said, 'But do carry on, my dear,' when I saw her saying part of the 'mono' with me – waited – and then started the verse again. I don't suppose anyone noticed, but even if they did, our little group of entertainers are much too nice to bring it to voice.

Anyway, that cutlery was never retrieved, and when, most thankfully, water was laid on in the village, the well was later filled in with all the unwanted and piled-up rubbish, and in another few years' time, maybe, perhaps thousands of years hence, when someone finds them, with some of my little lead soldiers nestling close by, they won't ever dream that their source was the feature of this true and likeable little episode.

The Whooping Cough

Norfolk, not unlike other rural communities, held its superstitions and folklore, and down through the ages ancient customs, beliefs and sayings were handed down from family to family and some are still retained even in this day and age. Folklore stems from the beginning of history and our early forefathers gave rise to many superstitions and some are practised more widely than it is realised. I remember Lucy, at the first sign of a new moon, venturing out into the garden and placing money in and amongst the produce – this was supposed to ensure the family would not want for money during the period of that moon until the next one formed its slender crescent. She was also very careful not to let me see where it had been placed.

I remember too that during the war I carried a wild rabbit's tail with me but this was lost with my battle dress at the front line casualty clearing station. However, my brother asked me about this and promptly produced another one which I then carried with me until the end of the war, when it did in fact moult. I know of men who still carry a potato from the first garden crop in a pocket until the next year and this, dried and flattened out, became as hard as stone and appeared to be not unlike a piece of granite – this prevented aches and pains, especially 'rumetics'.

Talking to the bees was considered to be favourable to the family fortunes and known as telling the secrets to the bees. Anything important such as marriages, births and deaths were told to the bees and failure to do this was considered most disastrous, especially if the bees moved off without having been told and the family would then suffer in consequence. All my generation can surely remember the cure for clearing warts and 'writs' was to rub the affected part with a piece of raw meat and then bury it in the soil and as the meat decayed so too were the blemishes supposed to disappear. Some would cycle for miles to visit a so called 'wart charmer' and the most remarkable coincidence was that in some cases they did lose sight of their unsightly appendages.

A 'burr' to the country man is the misty halo often enough seen around the moon and if this be large it is a sure sign of rain but if only small then the opposite is forecast. Bearing in mind and consideration that livelihoods were dependent on the weather, many beliefs were put into sayings and were common to Norfolk. Far burr – near rain, Near burr – far rain. March dry – good rye, April wet – good wheat. When it rains in the East with accompanying wind – it rains for twenty-four hours at least. The lengthy and narrow clouds of dark colour lazily floating low in the sky and very low are known as mares' tails and thus the saying, 'Water dogs and mare's tails make lofty ships have low sails'. The 'burr' around the moon is still a good weather forecaster and you will still hear the countryman say, 'We are in for a change, there's a "burrer" round the moon.' As I may have mentioned, Norfolk fishermen protected themselves against possible disaster at sea by wearing a single gold earring; in earlier days they wore amulets, one of which was a child's caul, the membrane sometimes found on a baby's head at birth, and this was worn around the neck believing it would prevent drowning.

All these traditional beliefs emanated from pre-Christian fertility religion, bearing in mind that man was closely bound to nature and aware of natural phenomena surrounding him; changing seasons affected his every day existence. As he worked on and with the land his beliefs were founded on observations and these later translated to spoken verses such as – 'A rainbow at morning be the shepherd's warning – a rainbow at night be the shepherd's delight' and who would give credence to a flight of wild geese or other like fowl in wintertime, intending to interpret this to be the sign of bitter weather to come. A little robin redbreast singing his heart out whilst sitting in the lower branches of a tree was the indication that bad weather was approaching.

Who would go to the extremes of wearing a dead toad around the neck to cure the pains of a sore throat and who would bake bread especially on Good Friday, keep it for the time when one of the family became ill and then feed it to that unfortunate person in the belief that having been baked on Good Friday it would thereby bring about therapeutics concerning a cure and remedial treatment? – our forefathers did! The eating of fruit in which a dead spider had been inserted was the infallible cure for ague, so too was the swallowing of those creepy crawly woodlice known as 'old sows' and 'millers' to the Norfolk man. There are many more which I suppose in the space of time will be forgotten for ever. If you feel queasy about reading this, well, how many times have you eaten the maggots which conceal themselves in raspberries and how many maggots have been swallowed when taking the bite from an apple and having swallowed them see the little beggars are swarming around the core?

How often do you see someone who spills salt, throw a pinch of that which has been spilled, over the shoulder? Even this is bound up with the previous two superstitions whose origins probably derive from the pagan sacrificial rites of the Saxons. Salt was buried in the ground and as this dissolved the complaint disappeared and taking into consideration that this commodity was very rare and extremely expensive it was regarded as being a magical element. Next time you spill salt and you too toss some over your shoulder remember you are practising this to keep at bay bad luck and the devil – if he is about to grab you around the waist you may even hit him in the eye.

Many are the times I have heard and read about covering a cut wound with a spider's web which has gathered dust in the corner, but then again did not Fleming take penicillin from mould which saved tens of thousands of lives, including mine, by combating dreaded gangrene.

I can now hear you all saying, but what about the whooping cough he remembered? So without further ado I will tell you. Where we lived at Clippesby our back door opened to the scene across the gardens to the front door of the house where Norma and Lennie Carter now reside. In my childhood, Russel and Doris Beckett lived there; he was the gardener for Doctor Tom Roydon, and a footpath led from their house to ours and various junctions branched off to other dwellings so as not to have to venture out on to the road. I was at home with whooping cough and one morning Mrs Beckett had traversed the footpath and was having a rare old 'mardle' with my mother, in which was mentioned about my complaint at

58

the time. I heard my mother say, 'In olden times they used to eat roasted mice and put a live 'dab' on the chest of a child.' When the fish died so the complaint disappeared. Of course these cures entered into the realms of sheer fantasy, but the boy 'Jimma' was too young at the time to understand this. Much later, I heard my mother telling my father, 'I don't know, Will, that boy has gone right off meat, all he seems to want is cheese on toast and eggs,' and I in my own childish way thought to myself, 'too true he has, no-one, not even my mother is going to make a blinking cat out of me.'

As I conclude, did you also know that women collected live snails, 'Dodderman's' and passed them over the hands of an affected child. These poor creatures, the 'Dodderman's' I mean, were then strung up inside the chimney breast to die, assuming that when they died so did the complaint.

Who would like to be born again and return to the eleventh century?

The Make-do and Mend

During the 1920s most Norfolk folk referred to 'Sunday best', 'second best' or 'working' when faced with the question of clothing, even down to the 'clorth cap' and even when they were past the Sunday best stage they were still not worn except for social events before being taken in for work.

The youngsters also had to be extremely clothes-conscious and on arriving home from a day's outing, Sunday school or Church, an immediate change was made in order to preserve those best togs in good condition. Another set of clothing was worn for school use before the blazer and grey shorts found their place in rural society. In some of the large families one set of best clothes was handed down three or four times subject to small alterations and it was often said of one child to another 'Them's mine when you have growed up.'

In the instance of footwear, this, even as today, was expensive but was then made of all leather and one pair would be resoled and heeled time and time again and even handed down until the uppers were past useful service. It was a constant trudge to the back of beyond at Burgh just outside the common land and marshes where lived a Mr Crane, the 'shumaker' and it was an after school or Saturday morning chore to take and fetch the family footwear to him. The soles of boots would be either tacked or stitched and if they were Dad's it would be 'an' three rows of double hobnails please, Mr

Crane!' I can picture him now as he worked away in his workshed, just inside the door and always seeking gossip news of the surrounding villages. 'How's old Mr so-and-so gitten on or hev Mrs.....got har bearby yit?' Without ever leaving his workshed he was well conversant and familiar with the comings and goings and various happenings over a wide area. Doreen, his schoolgirl daughter, was never short of company home from school as boots were made for walking and they wore out very frequently.

Clothes were sewn, darned and patched and sometimes there were more patches on a garment than that which remained of the original garment material; only then and reluctantly was it disposed of into the rag-bag hanging from a hook in the shed to await the coming of the rag-bottle-and bone man with his horse and cart and the heralding booming voice of 'Lumbo-lumbo,' when those patches would be handed over together with the rabbit skins off the nail on the wall for a few coppers. Everything had some value even when all value had seemingly disappeared. It is understandable why the clothes of a boy got into such a state considering the hedgerows and plantations were full of brambles and sharp thorns, also climbing trees and sliding down the sides of farm buildings on the sitting part of the short trousers.

When it came to socks, these were either of wool or cotton but mostly of wool and when a hole appeared or parts wore a bit thin, out came the darning needle until after many and repetitive darns it became extremely uncomfortable under foot, but even then I have seen the top of a sock salvaged and the foot re-knitted. Grannies and mothers were most adept in the art of knitting, and besides a refit to the foot of a sock, or a new sleeve to an ailing pullover, many garments were given as birthday or Christmas presents and very much appreciated by the recipients.

Good material which survived from coats and jackets retained its usefulness, as it was washed, cut into strips and placed away in the shed and later, when sufficient had been collected, a sack was opened up down one side and at the bottom, and with every other strand removed it became a ready-made canvas for a household rug. A sack was readily obtainable as almost everything was delivered in them: sugar, spices, corn, beans, rice and pulses to name just a few. Although it took many months of painstaking pegging away during the evenings, a beautiful rug was the end product, admired by all. With its various colours forming scrolls, diamonds, ovals, triangles or whatever desired, the household was proud of its newly fashioned and very useful commodity. Quite a few families made these piece rugs from time to time for their own use but some were sold as surplus to requirements and a good profit was made, because when well put together this type of rug, although heavy, was very much sought after and gave many years of good floor service.

Those of us who remember the so-called 'bad old days' must sometimes wonder if there were not some good in them after all, when we remember our winter months which always seemed to produce a heavy fall of snow and hard frosts. From Clippesby and Billockby we walked the nearly two miles to school as did other children in other parts of the county. The Hudson family of Clippesby walked to and from the school at Stokesby which was also a long distance. Many times the snow came over and above our knees but on reaching school we found the caretaker had made a clearance of the playground and had lit the fires to warm the large high-ceiling classrooms. Our teachers travelled from Martham and Great Yarmouth and either partly cycled or walked or took to horse and cart, but nevertheless arrived at the school.

At home we had light from our oil lamps and warmth from the wood and coal provided for and put by from the previous three quarters of the year, which proved to be good husbandry. Steam traction engines belching smoke, steam and flying sparks, cleared the roads with powerful ploughs and the horses drawing large-wheeled carts were able to move about.

Today, Friday 8th February 1991, much more than half a century having passed by, as I type this story I listen to Norfolk radio reeling out the number of schools closed, practically every one in the whole county, because the coaches, cars and trains are snowbound. It is a well-known fact that it only needs a small amount of snow to fall and then compact on our roads to render the movement of all our transport inoperable. Also, there are not now any steam-engined trains with scrapers bolted to their fronts to push through and clear the railway lines. In addition, no lengthmen are available as in the old days to clear the points from obstruction.

It is also a stark fact that our entire nation is becoming increasingly and almost entirely dependent on the use of electricity and, without it, railways, factories, shops and business premises are not able to function. Municipal and government departments are unable to operate and most would find it most difficult if, through the lack of electricity, that modern genius of technology, the computer, was cut off. Also, most homes where necessary measures have not yet been taken to provide alternative means would have no heat, light, power or cooking facilities. The sometimes cruel forces of the

61

elements we have to contend with could so easily play havoc with our electricity supplies, bringing everything to a grinding halt.

In our present brash age of speed and intolerance it appears we have forgotten the viciousness with which Mother Nature can suddenly strike and burden us with many types of disasters. To our detriment we have flaunted, spurned and insulted her, turning a blind eye, taking no heed of the legacy left to us by our forefathers.

Can yar Muthor Skin a Rabbit?

During the early 1920s there were several sayings which puzzled many a youngster, one of which has come to mind. When my father and grandfather were getting dressed to go out somewhere I would invariably ask where they were going and I would always get the same answer, 'Going to see a man about a dog' which was in effect a polite retort to mind my own business. Nevertheless, when they returned home I would rush outdoors excitedly expecting to be greeted with a bark and a lick from a puppy, as every boy of my age would have loved a dog to be his very own, but this was not to be and it took a long time for it to register that the answer given was a rebuff to not be nosey.

However, the old Norfolk saying of 'Can yar muthor skin a rabbit' was not a rebuff in itself but more of giving a snub when getting back at someone who was a little bit offish or in good old language, 'stuck up'.

Some mothers could and some could not, because skinning a bunny was one of the most tedious of tasks and had to be performed in the correct manner. To 'hulk' a rabbit was a different matter, this meant to take out the innards and was most probably mispronounced to the Norfolk tongue from the word 'Helkein' a derivation from the Greek language and meaning to draw. Some people used the word 'flear' when mentioning the skinning which is of course probably a misconception of the word 'flay'. I recall that on a very cold frosty morning people would utter, 'Cor it's enough to flear ya.' However, I learned to do both of these things and considered myself to be an expert from about the age of seven or eight, mainly because amongst other things, to me it meant that my red pillar box money holder was constantly being replenished with the rattling sounds of pennies and halfpennies with the odd small coins of silver. Readers will doubtless know that on some occasions rabbit skins afforded me the ticket entry to one of the picture palaces in Norwich and also extra pocket money.

I very quickly learned that collecting skins, whether they were rabbit, mole or whatever, was a lucrative endeavour which was proved beyond all doubt to be correct at the times when the 'look 'em up' man who collected lumber in the form of old iron, bottles, rags, skins and bones, made his call to the village. He would pay one old penny for a wild rabbit skin and perhaps three old pence for the skin of a tame rabbit which of course was very much larger in size. Many were the times I would be up to five shillings, an old crown, the richer following his visit and at the time this was a tidy sum of money for a young lad. To achieve most of this I would skin the rabbits found, and which had come to grief by the roadside verges and through other causes of injury.

At the same age I could also pluck, draw and dress a fowl, roast it and prepare a meal for my family. This knowledge came in most useful whilst I was serving with the Guards Armoured Division of the Army during the war when, whilst on training and manoeuvres as a newly formed Division to become battle proficient, we were a ravenous and hungry lot. Someone in the section would produce two or three live chickens and with a brace of the furry creatures which I was also adept in catching, I would do the necessary and over a wood fire out in the wilds of the Yorkshire Moors we would create the pungent aroma of the present day barbeques and we tucked into a very pleasant and hearty meal and I was recognised as a V.I.P. in my own right.

With regard to poultry, after being plucked the feathers were always retained in a sack and stored in the outside shed and when sufficient had been collected the points would be cut off, and this was, as can be imagined, a very tedious chore, and then placed in a cotton or muslin bag and sterilized in the heat of the oven after which very soft bolsters and pillows were made from them. A much larger bedroom item and requiring lots of 'fevvers' was the feather mattress. These were made by purchasing 'ticking' to sew up into a 'tick'. Readers of my generation will remember how very cosy and comfortable they were to rest the weary limbs and the aching back and to sleep on, and will remember and visualize the white ticking with a closely woven pale blue stripe and the whole of which was waxed on the inside to prevent the feathers poking through.

These were very comfortable indeed and were 'shook' up and shaken and turned almost every day. Most people find it very difficult to believe

63

and understand when I tell them that feathers were graded according to size and softness and that a pound in weight of soft downy feathers could realize about 1/6d whereas the coarser type would be only about 3d but then again the softer ones would be of a much greater volume in bulk. Even in this modern age of beautiful soft and comfy eiderdowns it is not really apparent to some that the very soft down obtained from the eider duck is of the very topmost grade and of course that is much more expensive, whereas that from the other species, although soft, is not of the same quality and therefore cheaper.

Nevertheless, feathers were always much more cosy and comfortable for bedtime and also the couches and cushions, than were the mattresses etc., manufactured from 'flock' material. Flock was constituted from old clothes, wools, rags and cotton waste being chewed up and finely shredded; this in time became lumpy and uncomfortable but could be remedied by having it recombed and the cords and buttons replaced. This material came from the efforts of the rag and bone man who after collecting from the various households then sold it to warehouses for recycling.

If any readers ever visit the town of Chichester, down the south coast, they will find a shop which still specializes and recovers old feather pillows and the like by using modern machinery. It is not well known that because feathers are densely packed into the tick when this is split open they will spill out everywhere, so the pillow is placed into the machine and closed before the tick is cut and the contents are then sterilized and blown into a new tick and sewn up. I have previously emphasised that my generation were of a very different moral and economical breed, just ask your Granny, obliged by necessity to make do and mend, cut corners and waste absolutely nothing. How many housewives in this age boil up the bones and carcases of joints and poultry and mixed with odds and ends of the coarser parts of vegetables concoct a sustaining soup which was not just a starter but sufficed for the main meal. What scraps were left over were used to feed poultry and boiled for pig swill, and waste was also collected from all hotels and restaurants for this purpose by pig breeders and keepers.

To-day, with much talk of the Third World not having sufficient food for their needs and their populations starving, have our readers ever noticed the vast amounts of food left on the plates by diners in hotels and eating places and then binned as rubbish. I am not suggesting that this should be frozen, packaged up and dispatched to them, but what a waste and a great

64

pity some people of our great nation will order more than they can possibly eat, thereby causing much comment.

I am not really a moaner, quite a nice amiable fellow really, but I am very conscious of waste and regard it as one of the many sins of this present day.

Returning to the skinning, plucking and whatever, this put me in great demand during later years and I was able to assist many families and the elderly when at Easter and Xmas they were given unplucked fowls and birds and the assortment of fare to be eaten on those days.

I did not really mind and as a limb of the law in those days I made good and friendly contacts and in helping the sturdy country folk they will never accept a favour without returning one and as a consequence of this my front porch was always scattered with seasonable produce and other items and I was forever being badgered by the local licensees, 'Will you please come and wipe the slate clean.' Then again, most of these drinks were passed on to the old village characters sitting in the corner of the pubs playing dominoes and sucking away at their smelly old pipes.

I sometimes wish I had retained some of the notes attached to the items I had to deal with, such as, 'Dear Sir, could you do this for me and Florrie, she don't like doing it as she think the eyes are looking at her.' Also notes such as, 'Dear Sir, can you make this so as I can put it in the oven because I don't think I have the stomik for it,' - meaning of course, would I make it presentable for cooking.

Such inspiring and memorable days.

The Thursdays

As a very small lad in the early 1920s, before reaching school age, I can remember when the morning milk was delivered around the various parishes by horse and milk float and a hand-bell was rung to announce that the milkman was in the vicinity. The time of day had to be considered by the housewife as to which hawker it was, but it was always round about ten o'clock when we got ours. The baker and grocer called at the door as a matter of course, but the fishman and milkman rang hand-bells to announce their presence and one would be obliged to go down to the road gate with a jug to collect. I was fascinated by the milkman and his float as this always struck me as being not dissimilar to a chariot, with shafts for the horse, a three foot high rounded front with the sides sloping down to the rear which was open to allow about three milk churns to be placed inside on the floor and for the milkman to step in and out. Half and pint aluminium scoops on long handles were used to dip into the churns and fill up the jugs which were proffered to the milkman to fill. This was a satisfactory service during the winter months or when the weather was cold and chilly but in the summer, or when hot, I remember my mother having to boil the milk to prevent it 'going off' as she used to put it. As everyone knows, there is nothing much worse than having a cup of tea with milk in it which is even just slightly on the turn.

This was also in the time when sugar came in sacks and was weighed out by the shopkeeper into half and pound bags which were manufactured of thick dark blue paper. Rice, flour, beans and other such commodities also arrived in sacks and were weighed out by the shopkeeper and almost every shop had a cat to keep down the mice. We didn't worry too much about little things like mice in those days.

Just over our garden fence a semi-detached house stood in Billockby and my grandfather had put up a chicken shed which was used partly as a demarcation line and I well remember a big whiskered man by the name of Jumbo Stone living in one end, and much, much later on, Jack and Mrs Dunham and Bertie and Gladys Parker at the other end. Whilst Jumbo Stone resided there he was employed by the council as a roadman and during the winter months would not return home before darkness had fallen, and consequently his groceries were delivered by a well-known grocery firm by the name of 'Clowes'. This firm used horse and traps for delivery purposes with their high, thin and tyred wheels and the groceries protected by a leather canopy surmounted on a wooden framework with straps and buckles fitted to keep it closed. On each side of the trap were situated brass candle lamps enclosed in glass surrounds and whilst the roundsman was attending to Jumbo's needs we thought it was great fun to blow out the candles and nip off the wick at the tip so that it was most difficult to light up again. Of course we tried this once too often and were forgetful of the fact that all horse drawn vehicles were equipped with those long and slender whips, much to our unfortunate but well-deserved soreness, when we were caught in the act. It was sharp and swift justice, the handing out of which taught us a lesson for the time being but never really did us any great harm.

However, before the days of cattle-floats and trucks, on a Thursday morning it was most important to shut all the gates leading to the road from the garden paths to each house as this was Acle Sale day, and bullocks, sheep and other cattle were driven along the roads, being picked up at various points from farms en route, and it was a most common sight to see a drover or 'bullock whopper' herding and driving these to market. The drovers were always dressed in the same fashion; you saw one and you had seen them all, with a light brown smock coat buttoned at the front, a cap or greasy trilby hat, brown market boots, and not forgetting the 'whopper' – usually a cane-type walking stick and the ever-faithful black and white Smithfield dog. Several herds of cattle would pass during the morning and also many of the solitary bullock or cow horse-drawn floats. Horse-drawn carts of all descriptions would pass by loaded with poultry and other small livestock, ending their first journey at either one or other of the saleyards and markets run by Waters and Son and Howlett and Edrich.

On the days when I was off school I would spend my whole time at the sales running the cattle pens, rabbit and poultry cages, and would always return home with at least a dozen eggs laid by the hens in the cages whilst waiting to be put up for sale. To get the eggs one would have to vie with the dealers who would just break the shells and swallow the egg raw – any cracked ones and I would do the same.

After the poultry and rabbits had been sold by the auctioneer they would be placed into wooden crates and as I stood looking on many is the time I have earned an old shilling when the dealer, taking the livestock from the cages, would yell out at me, 'Come you on and hold this here creart lid for us old partnar and when she's full up put that there hasp on and shove that there pin in!' The full crates would be loaded on to handcarts and pushed to nearby Acle station and a great number went off to London.

A large number of cattle were also transported to London by train, but these were also the days when all the local butchers had their own licensed slaughter houses and would attend the markets to select and buy of their own choice. The older residents of our own local area still talk about and savour the excellent pork sausages and joints of pork supplied by Charles Hall who had a butcher's shop one time next to Fleggburgh Post Office, and then later on moved to a site opposite the old Police House near to the Coffee Tavern on the main road, and long queues of patrons would wait patiently for a pound of his sausages.

I also remember my brother Freddie constructing a 4' x 2' x 1½' wood and wire-netting crate for his three-wheeled chain-cranked invalid chair. This would be placed on the footboard and roped to the chassis. During these days most people kept some kind of poultry or rabbits for the table and then sold the surplus, and during the week prior to a Thursday would call and book Freddie to take these to Acle sale, and I have known him to collect within a five-mile radius of our side of Acle and travel back and forth several times. He would place the stock in the cages and after the sale had finished collect the money due from the sales office and on a Thursday evening there would be a continual knocking at the door as callers came to collect their money and of course Freddie would get a percentage.

Since about the end of the Second World War all this has changed and, have you noticed, no livestock is sold at the Acle sales these days, and where there used to be two sale yards in close proximity to each other there is now only one.

Times have changed immensely and it would be almost an impossibility to drive cattle for long distances on our local roads today; one could just about imagine what it would be like along the Acle causeway or for instance along the seven-mile long Acle to Great Yarmouth straight, but years ago this had to be done and of course was done.

However, for tranquil thoughts and peace of mind I can still wander down the lanes of nostalgia, and reminisce how I spent some of the old shillings which I earned by giving the poultry dealer a hand, on sweets at Hudson's old wooden shop at Clippesby, and being asked by friends, 'Give us one of them thar cushies, and you can have a bite of my apple!'

Saturdays

On a Saturday during the late 1920s I would meet up with young Geoffrey Abel who lived in the semi-detached cottages at Billockby Corner. On occasions we would warm up by playing football, and then would play in the plantation opposite his house, climbing trees and, in season, bird's nesting and gathering hazel nuts which were plentiful. There were many more large trees than are evident today, and once aloft we could see, yet not be seen, and were privileged to an unobstructed survey over the marshes, fields and roads.

On a breezy day the many windmills would be pumping water from the marshes with their large sails revolving in never-ending motion. There was a peaceful tranquillity and quietness, only interrupted by the anxious and sometimes confused lowing of the cattle, of which there were many.

From our lofty perch we could easily see the river traffic almost from the Thurne to Acle Bridge, and would perchance sight the huge sails powering one of the few large black-hulled barges which plied their trade along the Bure from Great Yarmouth. If sailing towards the coast we would alternate in running and walking to Acle Bridge and watch it come up river and the bargee lower the massive mast and sail and quant up to and under

The Old Acle Bridge

the middle arch of the old bridge. We could not resist crossing the river by way of the narrow bridge parapet, giving not a thought to the danger involved: it was there setting a challenge to our boyish enthusiasm.

Often we could get a ride back by horse and tumbril or waggon, but sometimes a barge would sail from the Yarmouth direction, and walking along the river bank we would follow its progress round the bend of the river until opposite Clippesby, then, waving goodbye, would make our way over the marshes to home.

There were gates intersecting the variously owned marshes, but we would jump the dykes to add fun to our expedition. The dykes being of varied width and depth would be approached according to size. However, our fast or slow runs were often misjudged and would land us in the duckweed and other oddities.

The marshes were always lush and abundant with wild flowers and a beautiful posy of these picked on the way would not prevent mother from wielding the once very much used copper stick when we eventually arrived home, wet, muddy, and smelly. Still, these were happy, carefree days with free abandon, with Sunday School and Church on the morrow, and the eventuality of five more days at school before we could cut loose again. How we all hated the coming of Monday morning!

Sundays

On a Sunday during the late 20s there were no games or the usual activities which everyone enjoyed or were employed in during the week. Our Sunday School at Clippesby was held at the Church at I think about 10 o'clock, and we from the bottom of the village would walk along the main road, turn left into Hall Road and then along the footpath which ran in between the field and the hall pastures, into and through the small wood leading into the church porch. Jean and her family still use part of this walk even now.

However, a little respite for mischief had to creep in. Most folk will still remember the field gates at intervals along each side of the road, before the hedges and banks were obliterated, and when fields were an average 8-10 acres each. We would climb the gates and walk along the top rail from end to end. Also the Post Office telephone system was relayed by overhead wires attached to poles 45 yards apart, and the top cross arms were festooned with white insulating cups which were a target for our accurate stoning.

After Sunday School it was home for dinner and in season we always had our sweet in reverse order by way of the orchard at South House farm, where there was always an abundance of all kinds of tree fruit.

Dinner over, and in the winter months, if the weather was fine, young John Drake and I would cycle to Great Yarmouth and back via Caister-on-Sea, take the ozone along Yarmouth front, and return home by the Acle New Road. Sometimes it would be to Hemsby or Potter Heigham and Hickling Broads. Even at schoolboy age we were both experienced in cycle repairs and carried tools and puncture outfits in the event of mishaps.

Stopping at the old Acle Bridge we would carry out our customary and crazy exercise of crossing the span by way of the parapet, cross over and back along the other side. The parapet was only about 10 inches wide, neither of us could swim, and our minds were shut to the fact that under the middle arch the water depth was 12-15 feet.

During the spring and early summer, almost everyone from Clippesby and Billockby would take up leisurely strolling. Parents and children would saunter along the causeway, meeting and chatting to other families and then rendezvous at Acle Bridge. Watching the sailing boats and eating ice-cream was the order of the day. No walking along the bridge parapet, mind you, especially with parents present.

Back home in time for tea, then the inevitable horn gramophone and records in the evening. 'Silver threads among the gold' – 'When the golden sun sinks in the West' – anyone feeling the pangs of nostalgia? The older males would resort to the old Reading Room at Billockby where a nice fire would be burning, around which cards were played, not for money in those days, but for matches. They also had a small billiard table and a dart board. Not much according to present day values, but reasonably happy.

These were fairly quiet days, in fact. Almost every village had a football and cricket team, and then there were the heinous offences of poaching and riding a bicycle without lights, and of course, snowballing the schoolmaster!

Winter Nights in the 1920s

Late November and into December brought dark miserable mornings and equally dark and misty, foggy evenings. During the week it was usually cold and wet walking to school, and returning in the late afternoon it was almost dark on arriving home again. There was no outside activity after school but most parents usually found us household chores to keep us occupied. My jobs were to chop the kindling wood and light the fire, fill the coal bucket

71

and place sawn logs by the fireplace. The oil lamp had to be filled with paraffin and lit ready for the evening. This was the main form of lighting and almost every household relied on this type of lamp. In addition there were candles and candlesticks to light the way about the house, but mostly used to light the way to bed, and each member of the family would own their own candlestick. Electric light didn't arrive till about 1936. Another job allocated to me was to cut the bread for tea. Although young I could cut very thin and even slices from a loaf without it breaking to pieces.

On a Saturday it would be into the farmyard, where by this time the strawstacks were being used to bed down the cattle in the yards, and it was great fun climbing the stacking and then sliding or jumping down to a lower level. Also, in the barn the cattle feeder would be using the hopper cutter to chip up the swedes for the cattle to feed on, and these were very succulent and tasty indeed, but a tummy ache was to follow. A climb along the side walls of the cattle yard, a shin up the gable end of the big barn, and then sitting astride the ridge would give a great panoramic view over the immediate neighbourhood and the surrounding fields and marshes. From here, when we got cold, we adjourned to the plantation at Billockby corner where, if we shuffled and searched amongst the leaves, hazel nuts could still be found.

Just after tea I would sometimes visit a friend of mine living on the top road at Billockby, George Cooper by name, but nicknamed 'Jewson'. About the same age as myself, he was most unfortunate to have had asthma, and because of this was unable to attend school, but, on his easier days he was able to get about fairly well and we would play together. One old penny each would enable us to buy a packet of 5 Woodbines and there was many a glow in the darkness and a furtive cough thereabouts. My mother used to say to my father, 'Will! have you taken my matches again?'

I remember one such evening it had turned dark suddenly and because I was somewhat afraid of walking past the plantation alone because of the potential 'hikey sprites', and the myriad of strange noises where even the wind rustling the treetops and bushes made ominous swishing noises, he reluctantly agreed to walk home with me. It is hard to imagine that such a pleasant and happy place which afforded us such joyous surroundings during the day should be so frightening once darkness had fallen, when one's senses were very much alert to the uneasy rustling, and the sudden screech of an owl could render one's blood to crushed icicles. However, on reaching my gate he was then nervous of going back alone and in the end after long and hard deliberation we decided to accompany each other to a rough point half way along the plantation and then run very fast in our respective directions. Arriving home with a fast-beating heart, on going to bed that same night, with the candle flickering madly, I got on my hands and knees and looked under the bed to make sure no one was lurking underneath there.

Meeting next day, we were both very brave – 'Nothing to it!' 'I wasn't really frightened, were you?' 'Bet you so-and-so wouldn't dare do it!' Nevertheless, Saturday has passed by again, and later this evening, Sunday, I will wend my way to St Margaret's, Fleggburgh, to sing with the choir. It will be dark again on the way home, but I shall be all right; haven't I been to church? But for all my complacency I shall run like nobody's business, and believe me, I'll take some catching!

The Old Chapel

In the late 1920s when I was about 9 or 10 years of age I often played in the old chapel which stood at the bottom of our garden, adjacent to the road. It had been de-consecrated and I would find my way inside through a broken window. An old harmonium had been left discarded and I found that by pedalling furiously I could obtain about five notes and these were sufficient to see me through the hymns which I sang. In between hymns I would preach to an imaginary congregation. Whilst singing away and playing my five notes, the laughing face of Mrs Nellie Turner, who resided close by, would appear through one of the windows, and being a very kind and considerate lady, would give me two old pennies and sometimes a shiny threepenny bit. (No, no, you have it all wrong – not to STOP singing, but to carry on!) We got on very well together, and when I left home at the ripe old age of fifteen and a wee bit, I always made a special call on her whilst on furlough, to share a pot of tea in her very small back kitchen. We always enjoyed a right good 'mardle' and our conversation would wander back to the singing in the chapel. Isn't it a great pity that some of the very nicest and special people cannot live on for ever? To her I was always 'the boy Jimma'; and the memories still linger on.

Some time later a Mr Allen ('Buss') bought the old chapel and we became great friends. I watched and helped him renovate the old building

73

into a sitting-room and bedroom, and carried bricks inside whilst he built the fire place and chimney stack. When completed it became a cosy little nest for him and his wife to spend their last days, and I was a regular visitor during which time he taught me to do many things, one of which was the cutting and making of genuine gypsy pegs. (Any orders forthcoming will be executed with the greatest efficiency!)

Arriving home later on, after a spell away, 'Buss and his lady' had passed on, and the new residents were 'Jolt' Parker and his wife, Nellie, who was a daughter of the Allens. They extended the property very modestly with the construction of a small kitchen, and later on a small static caravan close by the side. Both resided here for quite a few years and I often spoke to and visited 'Jolt' on my visits home.

However, when Jolt and Nellie passed on, the old property was sold, and believe it or not was given two or three splashes of paint, and the window frames were slightly modified and it became a holiday home for a family and their relatives and friends from Essex. This continued for a few years, after which it was sold again and stood empty for a long, long time. The ravages of both winter and summer played their part in almost rendering the old place to the same condition as it had been in my boyhood days before 'Buss' Allen came along. It was sold once again but no use was made of it and subsequently it was pulled down.

Very much like our own existence, buildings come to life when the footings and the very first brick is put down, and as time elapses so we together also deteriorate, and in the end only photographs remain. As I pass by now I notice all that remains is the chimney stack, which almost a life time ago I helped to construct, later sitting by a cosy fire, cutting, shaping and creating 'gypsy pegs'.

Somewhere I have a snapshot of the old chapel, but cannot bring it to hand; probably the only reminiscent essence it now has is of a once loved and revered building where devout Christians knelt in prayer and like the structure are now at rest and obliterated.

I feel somehow I have witnessed the end of an era, and wonder if in the future when there is a full moon, and wisps of mist are creeping and billowing over the marshes, someone passing by will hear, as if from nothingness, the strains of crystal clear melodies and a young voice echoing 'The Lord's my shepherd', and 'Rock of Ages', accompanied by the wheezy musical notes emanating seemingly from nowhere... I wonder!

PEOPLE

Nobby and his Old Dicky

When anyone mentions a 'Nobby' it has to be said that the surname everybody immediately brings to mind is Clark; in fact, in the Army each and every one is and remains a Nobby regardless of whether he be a Field Marshal or enlisted boy. 'Dicky' is unmistakably and for ever Norfolk lingo for 'donkey', and many a Norfolk lad has been laughingly tormented with the old adage, 'Heve yar Farthar gotta dikky bor?' and not being as dull and mentally unreceptive as purported to be, would often cause a rumpus by answering, 'Yis, an he's looken fer a fule to ride on ut. Are you gearm?'

Howsomever, back in the early 1920s, we had a Nobby Clark in Clippesby, living just about forty yards along the road from our house towards Billockby Corner and the allotments, in a very small clay and flint-walled cottage. It was one up and one down, with some outhouses and the usual detached, as far from the house as possible and whatever-the-weather retreat, up the cinder-covered garden path. Nobby had no stairs, and went to bed by way of a little trap-door in the ceiling, reached by a short ladder, obviously nothing like nor a patch on today's standards or values, but nevertheless, this was home to Nobby; and during fine evenings and especially on a Sunday he would sit on his plank of wood seat, using an old cornsack folded over as a cushion, which was supported between the house wall and the road fence, where he could take note, rest and 'mardle'.

I forget where Nobby worked but in accordance with others I think it was on a farm either at Oby or Thurne, and to commute to and fro he used a 'dicky' and cart for transport. Now of course the young rascals of the village, myself included, soon got to know the old 'dicky' was most partial to juicy carrots and little sweetmeats, so when Nobby returned from work we would position ourselves spaced out on each side of the road, and who could blame the poor old animal for just zig-zagging along the road from one side to 'tother'? Naturally enough, all the rein-pulling, tugging, swearing and shouting didn't worry the old 'dicky' one little iota, and Nobby obviously became utterly annoyed because he eventually equipped himself with a long-stemmed whip – not for the 'dicky', but for us – and I can assure you when he lashed out I was on the receiving end more times than I care to admit, and I did quite a bit of hopping about on one foot.

The old 'dicky' was stabled in one of a group of sheds on the top road at Billockby, and in fine weather we would on occasions let him out and have a ride round the little paddock. Many were the times when he wouldn't budge, but when feeling inclined to do so would kick out with his back legs, arch his back and topple us over his head, and having done this would let off a couple of brays and a roar as if to tell us, 'I'll show you young warmins what's what!' Very often, although he would come out friendly enough, we couldn't get the old devil back into his stable, and one of us with tongue in cheek would knock on Nobby's door and 'haller' out, 'Yar ole dicky's out agin, Nobby, an he's a hully rampagin round that there fild.' Nobby was no fool; he knew what it was all about, and to let the 'old sleepen dorgs keep on a-snoren.'

However, I did just once to my knowledge fall into his amiable esteem. One Saturday afternoon I was on the top road when on glancing down towards the earth verge I saw what looked like a folded piece of green paper and on picking it up immediately went goggle-eyed: but when unfolding it, I became even more so, because what I had found was to me a small fortune – a ten shilling note folded within a £1 note. They were wet and soggy, but represented a man's wages and would fund a family for a week, with a little to spare. At the time I was sorely tempted. What little boy wouldn't be? I thought of all the sherbet bags, gob-stoppers, aniseed balls, liquorice boot laces and such luxuries as bottles of ginger beer, but the instinct of a good family upbringing rallied above my selfish reasoning and I took my find home to my mother.

Two or three nights later, just after tea, there was a knock on the back door and when I heard my father say, 'Come in, Mr Clark,' I nearly had kittens and turned frozen cold and immediately sought a retreat behind my grandfather, sitting in his tall Victorian wooden arm chair. My mind ran rampant. I couldn't for the life of me think what I had done to justify this visit and could only imagine the old 'dicky' had pegged out and I was being blamed for it. We didn't have computers in those days but I can assure everyone that I had in a matter of minutes collated more than a fair number of pardonable excuses to last until I left school. But Nobby came in smiling and, as per the custom of those long-off days, the tobacco pouch was handed round to fill one's pipe with as much of the weed as could be rammed into the bowl.

What actually had happened was that my family had waited for the village 'grapevine' to bear fruit, and it came to pass that poor old Nobby had lost his week's wages. He offered me five shillings and I remember my hand went out like a shot but I was not allowed to accept or take it, being

77

told later that Nobby was a poor old man and there was no substance in the old saying of 'Finders is keepers'. I somehow made myself understand that this was right and just, but on the Sunday following whilst going up to church I stoned more than my fair share of the telephone post insulation cups, trying to appease my dislike of all grown-ups.

I suppose it would be about a year or so later when Nobby died. On the Saturday morning when he vacated his little cottage for the very last time I was kicking my heels outside our road gate when I saw his plain wooden coffin being removed to the sidecar of a motor cycle combination. It was securely tied and roped to the sidecar; the machine kick-started and he was away on his last earthly journey. The roads in Clippesby during these days were uneven, with pot holes, so that the coffin swayed, tipped and rolled, and not without sound reason did an overwhelming surge of disbelief stir within me, but then, what could I have done? As people repeatedly said, 'Times are hard.'

I was reminded of a song which Georgie Cooper (Jewson) and I would sing together, with him playing his accordion, namely 'Little Jimmy Brown', but on his last day he was fortunate to be honoured with tears from his family and friends, in the presence of a congregation of people who cared. Not so for Nobby, just the parson, a grave digger, and the man on the motor cycle combination – not even the fragrance of a flower or the solace of the wonderful hymn 'Just as I am without one plea'. I somehow felt honoured being the little boy at the garden gate to see him off on his last poignant and bumpy farewell. I was just old enough to understand when I asked if I could see the donkey that he, the cart and the harness had been sold to reimburse the council for funeral expenses.

Each time as I pass along the road and through the village of my birth and upbringing, my being is wholly engrossed with the nostalgic and tender golden memories of the hard but happy family ties, the wonders and beauteous gifts of nature embracing the marshes, woods and countryside, the joys and escapades of my sometimes over-zealous and exuberant misdemeanours; and yet if the clock could be turned back I am conscious of a hesitancy to fulfil the yearning of doing it all again.

The Village Blacksmith

It all seems a long time ago, many snowflakes have fallen and indeed many swallows have braved our summers, but have gone, and myriads of adventures, achievements and even disillusionments which have filled one's life have appeared like the evening mists rolling over the marshes, only to disappear and evaporate and be swept silently away when the rays of the sun first break through - to where? Yes, where have they gone, those dreams, those fleet digressions of life, which we all at some time or other have promised ourselves we would cherish forever, but which have been forgotten, they having been swept away like a nonentity.

Fortunately, not all is forgotten. Returning to my schooldays I remember the Saturday mornings, when on most occasions I was up and about fairly early and hastened to the farm. In those days a farm was a hive of intense activity, before the tractors came along and polluted the countryside with the eye-tingling paraffin fumes and when horses reigned supreme, cattle of all species filled the enclosed yards and there was always much to occupy one's time and energy. Normally, this was the day when if a horse needed shoeing, it visited the blacksmith at Acle to have new shoes fitted, so it could be ready for work on the Sunday morning. The horse at South Farm, Clippesby, would be walked to Acle with just a rope halter and a sack thrown over its back, so I would be able to ride there and back.

A blacksmith's shop on all occasions was a veritable wonderland of bits and pieces of everything, odds and ends of that which at some time in the future might come in useful. The anvil was mostly positioned at the foot of the fire grate with its clutter of working irons, numerous horseshoes already fashioned and shaped, were seen suspended from racks on the walls, broken implements to be made good and always, close to the anvil, the copper of water in which to cool the finished products. That which invariably held my fascination was the fire in its shallow but proportionate basket grate, with the very small cut hard coals and above which and to the back were the bellows operated by a long wooden handle which was pumped up and down to supply the air and assist the deep red glow and excessive heat of the coals necessary to reduce metal to an almost liquid state. The bellows were very similar to those of organs, except probably just a bit larger and the handle always sported a spent horn from a cow or bullock!

79

Outside and propped against the walls could be seen a clutter of harrows, ploughs, assorted wheels and farm paraphernalia and never without the round iron templates on which the iron tyres were moulded to wooden-spoked wheels a few feet from the door.

Normally, a blacksmith, wearing heavy leather boots plentifully protected with several rows of hobnails, thick corduroy trousers and then, over all, a thick leather apron split up the middle, would work with shirt sleeves rolled to the elbows, and would never be seen not wearing the wide leather bands strapped to his wrists to prevent ligament strain. When applying heat to any article he also managed the bellows and was virtually one-handed, and I suppose, in a way, always pleased to see an eager-eyed youngster who would work the bellows for him. Anyway, I always came away with an old 1d. and sometimes 2d. in addition to having the mug of cocoa.

The blacksmith at Acle at this time was a John Wilkerson and after the smithy closed I suppose it was this man's son who then took over the site as a cycle dealer and repairer. I would go to him whenever either side crank on my bike became bent, which was pretty often, and to this day I chuckle when I remember asking 'Please Mr Wilkerson, will you bend my crank straight' and this was achieved by applying a large adjustable wrench to it and exerting a bit of pressure. All trace of the blacksmith's shop disappeared in the early 1930s but there is still a Wilkerson on the site and trading as a household goods shop, probably a third or fourth generation, and in addition, on part of the land where once stood the cycle shop, there now stands a butcher's shop, situated just a bit further back. I can still recall gazing at the brand new three-speed cycles on display, priced at £2 to £3.10s. and thinking to myself, 'I could have one of them if I collected 480 rabbit skins', but then again, even at the age I was then, common sense prevailed and I comforted myself with the thought that I already had a bike, even though it was a 'bitza', which took me as far as I needed to travel and back.

Just past the blacksmith's, on the acute bend which is still there, and just prior to entering the street, stood the ancient brick house, opposite to which, was the baker's shop and both are still there, but the baker's shop has been renewed and has changed hands several times. So too, has the garage which was then owned by Arnold G. Smithdale, motor engineers and repairers. Along to the street, and that shop which is now the Co-op was owned by G. H. Rix & Son, grocers, haberdashery and oddments. The school was further down the street near the church, but this has now had its day, and just further on are the two saleyards – Waters & Son and Howlett & Edrich where, whilst on holidays, I spent many happy hours.

Old Church Schoolroom, Clippesby

Most of the shops during these early days provided services for the farming community and I remember, at the same time as visiting the blacksmith's, sometimes calls would be made to the saddlery establishments and horse chandlers where harness was bought and repaired. I suppose that one of the visits to Acle which I remember most was the one to Herbert Cripsey, the hairdresser, and having to sit and wait my turn to take the chair to have, as the old saying went, 'my ears put back' and having to pay an old 6d. for the privilege.

Immediately opposite the blacksmith's was the well-known shop of George Thompson, house furnisher, ironmonger, motor engineer, motor car garage, petrol pumps and cars for hire. I well remember I often had to shop here for my family and this was the shop where we purchased our fireworks. I can still envisage Mr Thompson, a tall man of proportionate build who mostly wore a tweed suit, gold watch chain with baubles dangling from the waistcoat pockets, and always a bow tie and trilby hat.

His old shop and the adjoining builders' yard are now just a memory and a cul-de-sac of houses and modern shops have taken over. However,

81

you may be surprised with one snippet of true information – to shoe one cart horse in 1911 was 2s. 4d., repairing a harrow 3s. 6d. and to trim a horse's hoofs on the farm cost 4s. 0d. Sweat and toil needing strength and know-how culminated into a profit of about 16s. 0d. each week.

At school there were many titters arising from the furtive gatherings of both boys and girls, who in small groups in the extremities of the playground, held sessions, during which ribald jokes were swapped at the expense of the blacksmith, but this was just one part of growing up, to hear, listen and decide which path one trod to shape one's life and interests.

To and from Acle was most enjoyable and interesting, I could watch the activities on the marshes from horseback height, the numerous cattle feeding, wild life abounding, birds, bees and butterflies of all hues and colours, the windmills with sails lazily turning and the unchanging panorama was all before me, and perchance, I might even have glimpsed a tall mast bearing the massive black sail and flying a long pennant streamer.

Long Arthur

Along the Acle causeway during the 1920s as a young lad I would often see men of untidy and unkempt appearance, and mostly with shaggy matted beards, trudging along and carrying a rolled-up blanket slung over one shoulder and secured with binder twine. A stout stick over the other shoulder supported a bag or sack in which were carried their worldly possessions and goods. They were saddled with the unbecoming tag of tramps or loafers but later on these words were deleted from the vocabulary of most folks and they then acquired the more fashionable name of 'gentlemen of the road'. These men were people of the workhouses of the day and I knew there were such places as these at Swainsthorpe along the road to Ipswich from which place they would tramp to Bowthorpe in Norwich, now the West Norwich Hospital. From here a long tramp to Lingwood just outside Acle and thence to Northgate in Great Yarmouth which is also now a hospital. At each stopping place they were deloused and bathed, with clothes fumigated and, if needed, a clothes change would be made. A work task had to be performed in repayment for rough meals and shelter after which they would again take to the road.

Whilst on the road they would sleep rough in woods and plantations, but the most luxurious of abodes was a nice comfy straw stack from which straw could be teazed out making a hole, the loose straw being pulled back to conceal the opening.

Some people in the villages would bear sympathetic feelings towards them and during the late afternoon on calling at some houses they would ask for and receive enough tea and sugar to make a brew over a small wood fire. My grandfather often handed over a shilling coin and enough of that odious and evil-smelling 'bacca' called Churchman's Counter Shag, to help put taste into and supplement the short fag ends picked up along the road. I never could find any but it was said that various marks and signs were left to provide information to those following along later, which people were of a friendly nature towards them and also which ones to avoid.

I remember one such tramp called 'Long Arthur' simply because the name suited his stature in every respect. He was roughly six feet and four inches tall, skinny and resembling a marsh dyke-jumping pole and of course as kids of my day were cheeky and saucy and in some cases very cruel in their actions, we sometimes cheeked and mimicked him.

I recall that one day when with Geoffrey Abel who lived in the old stone cottage, now demolished, at the apex of the Clippesby to Billockby road junction as approached from Acle river bridge, we saw 'Long Arthur' tramping towards us. We got on to the marsh where we thought we would be safe with a wide dyke and five feet of water between us.

'Long Arthur' got more than a wee bit angry and threw clods of earth at us and also stones but we never thought for one moment that on reaching the next gate he would climb over and chase us – but he did. My goodness did we run, and how, fearing the worst if he caught us.

We crossed from one marsh to another by using the 'ligger', a plank placed across the width of a dyke to cross over safely. On crossing over the next dyke we lifted the 'ligger' and pulled it to our side of the water. We kept on running and were much gladdened when on looking back our chaser had decided to return to the road. We waited and watched him out of sight and then realised we had to replace the 'ligger' back across the dyke so as not to evoke the wrath of the marshman who would undoubtedly have found out who we were and would have stopped our playing on the marshes in the future. We found it much more heavy than we thought and whilst trying to replace it I fell into the dyke and with the black mud, duckweed, rotting reeds and other vegetation mixed with the methane gas exuding from the mud I really did smell badly. We managed to replace the

'ligger' and made our way home through the plantation at Clippesby corner and then I went over the allotments and across the field, through the gap in the hedge and along our garden path. My mother must have detected the obnoxious odour of her youngest offspring because she met me over the 'troshel' and her face bore a look of utter despair and disgust.

Nevertheless, off the nail on the outside wall of the house came the tin bath, the copper in the scullery was filled with water and the fire lit underneath it. About half an hour later I had been scrubbed clean, and I do mean scrubbed, when once again for a little while I was as shiny as a packet of new pins, and sent up to my bedroom with a resounding 'ding of the lug'.

Sitting, gazing out of my bedroom window over a closing afternoon I looked out over the cold misty scene of the panoramic beauty of nature and I watched the cattle, their coats in colours of red, black and white in all variations of patches, stripes, spots and blotches munching away at the lush marsh grass and every now and again one would cough loudly setting up a chain of reaction from the others from Upton to Fishley and Thurne to Ludham.

Suddenly, with huge mast and black sail and flying its long streamer pennant, a wherry peeped into view and with its majestic slow manoeuvring along the river Bure the lone wherryman would negotiate his large craft around the bends of the winding river and moor up for the night just on the Bridge Inn side of Acle bridge where his needs would be sustained. Later on he would be enjoying a well-earned pint of old ale which, after being suitably warmed in a saucepan on the pub fire or by the insertion of the tip of a red hot poker, would re-kindle the sparkle to his tired features. With this, in company with a hunk of bread and cheese and two or three pickled onions, he was a happily replenished man.

All the night sounds and screeches of barn owls as they hunted for their prey nearby would not disturb him in his deep sleep induced by a hard day's work and the warmth coming from his small cubby-hole cabin with its little coal-fire stove. King George the fifth was totally unaware that at least one of his faithful subjects was well satisfied with his meagre lot.

He would hoist his large black sail again when from the Acle marshes the greylag goose trumpeted his dawn call and, slowly but surely, as the breeze assisted him in his slow passage along the waterway, he was once again on his never-ceasing journey, associating himself with the wildlife that shared his existence.

From the bottom of the stairs a call from my mother shattered my reverie, 'Come on, tea's ready'. Going downstairs I said hello to my father who was just home from work and to my grandfather sitting in his chair by the fire and once again I detected that quiet reassuring smile and sparkle in his eye as much as to say, 'Don't worry, you are a chip off the old block'.

There was that lovely aroma of roast beef and Yorkshire puddings with the assorted vegetables on the table. I hashed my potatoes into a mountain, made a tunnel through which diced carrots and peas floated through on a river of gravy. Two Yorkshire puddings on either side sufficed for river banks and once again I visualized that huge black sail gliding gracefully over the skyline. A sharp command of 'Either eat it, or the cat will' spoilt my mountain tunnel and river bank and put an end to the carrots and peas sailing through on the gravy river.

Not long after this and as a further punishment I was packed off to bed, and, looking under the bed just in case 'Long Arthur' the tramp had by some means got underneath there, I jumped into my feather-mattressed boat and was soon in the land of nod.

What a day!

The Gypsies

When I reached the age of five years, it was the custom of the early 1920s to commence school. There were no getting-to-know-you preparatory sessions, no pre-school nursery groups to pave the way to protect us from the horrible trauma of being pitched in at the deep end, and one did for the first day or two almost drown in the tears of utter misery until the new experience thrust upon us levelled out and a foundation of friends was formed.

My route to school was a three hundred yard walk to the Loke down which I made my way to meet up with the main road and the other children from Billockby, and thence the long trudge in all weathers to the school at Fleggburgh.

The Loke is very much the same today as it was then except for the tall hedges and several oaks which have disappeared. George Cooper (Jewson) and I were responsible for one hedge being missing and it never really recovered from the time when we set the Loke on fire whilst trying to bake potatoes in a hole on the side of a bank. (No vandalism or malice was intended but just an unfortunate breeze suddenly awakened to curtail the innocent pleasures we were contemplating at the time. See page 98)

Just about thirty-five to forty yards along the Loke from the junction with the Clippesby Road and immediately prior to the first bend, there has in my memory always been a small triangular parcel of land upon which at some time in the 'dear dead days beyond recall' there had most probably been a stone cottage. No-one seemed to know anything about this, but I remember seeing decaying planks of wood which covered a filled-in hole, the top of which was about five feet in diameter and which had at one time served as a well for drinking water.

It was on this small piece of land that once or twice yearly, one and sometimes two gaily-painted horse-drawn gypsy caravans stopped over

86

Easter and then again at the beginning of autumn for a period of a few days. Their presence was most inconvenient to us who used the Loke, because we were told to keep away from gypsies as they would take away naughty boys and girls. Most of us didn't have to search our souls to any depth to know that if we did venture within their midst, we were 'gonners' and would without doubt disappear without trace.

What a time we lived in, for if it wasn't the gypsies intending to take us, it would be the 'hob goblins', whoever they were, and failing them, the 'hikey sprites' on the marshes who were not too friendly by all accounts, and then there were the tramps in the woods. Can you wonder why we now resemble nervous wrecks? It is a wonder we ever survived. Possibly we were only bad in a good way after all! Anyway, whilst the encampment remained within our little community, we had to avoid the Loke on going to school and take the long way round which meant a good half mile extra to trudge by way of Billockby corner and past the plantation where much to our relief the tramps had not yet awakened.

News spread round the villages like wildfire and all movable chattels were packed away and sheds locked, and those householders who kept hens, other breeds of poultry and tame rabbits were very much on the alert. Any slight unusual noise during the night was immediately investigated and the smelly old paraffin oil hurricane lamp was kept at the ready. The women in their long flowery dresses sweeping the ground, and sporting large dangling ear rings, carried woven baskets; these were filled to the top with charms, pegs, cottons, tapes, pins, varied dried herbs and flower sachets, and they canvassed from door to door, always echoing the inevitable cries of 'Cross my palm with silver and good fortune will come to you.'

My little school friend Muriel Gowing lived in the stone cottage near to the Loke entrance, where the Tubbys now reside, and her garden stretched right down to the corner where the gypsies were, and through the thick boundary hedge we would watch unnoticed as they skinned rabbits and plucked the 'long-tailed pigeons' following which these were placed on a long skewer which rested between forked rods placed either side of a wood fire. Sometimes they would joint the rabbits and place them in a hanging cauldron and, adding sliced turnips and swedes, the cooking smells would permeate through to us. But for the unfounded fables and superstitious talk, we would have loved to be able to join in with them.

The horses which pulled the caravans, the coloured breed which we called 'piecrusts', were on long tethered lines and munching away at the lokeside grass. The dogs – they always appeared to favour the same breed – were lean and hungry-looking lurchers, a cross between collie and greyhound renowned for their speed and running powers, and being able to chase and catch a hare with ease. Rabbits were a very minor problem. They were usually sleeping under the caravans, resting up after the previous night of prowling for game and whatever came within sight.

A few days later the gypsies were gone, and coming home from school in the afternoon I would rush home for the wheelbarrow, broom and shovel to collect that which the horses had left behind, to enrich the soil around my grandfather's roses and daphne bush. Being a country lad I was bound to notice the wisps of hay left by the horses – there was always a huge stack of hay on each of the two nearby farms and who could deny the animals their favourite supper?

Also in the ashes of the wood fire there were pretty coloured feathers partly burned but not completely destroyed so as not to be able to define the source they had come from; without doubt those gypsies lived high and well according to our standards. Of course there was no evidence of hare or rabbit skins as these would be kept and sold to a 'look 'em up' for a few pence later on.

Anyway, we could now frequent the Loke again as a short cut to school and the wild animals that ventured abroad at night could now do so with comparative safety because gone were the dogs, gin traps and snares plus the purse nets which for a short period had impeded their progress. In a short while the patches of fire-stained soil produced a fine cover of young fresh green grass and once again the Loke reverted to the secluded, tranquil and pleasant venue down which to wander, enjoy, browse and search for the friendliness of that delightful fullness which nature provides.

Further to the previous-mentioned covered and filled-in well, if you can recall quite a time ago I told you how my very good friend 'Buss' Allen bought and renovated the old chapel in which, after completion, he and his wife resided happily during their twilight days, and I also highlighted his activities as a handyman. Once again I must tell you more about this remarkable old timer, how he sized up this small parcel of loke land, unwanted and desolate, and envisaged in his mind's eye the future prospects of a neat vegetable and flower garden. Firstly the well had to be dug out to its original depth of about 15-20 feet at which depth once again the water appeared. A brick surround surmounted by a roof, an old mangle wooden roller with handle attached, a length of rope with a bucket on the end, and he had water at hand without the bother of fetching and carrying it from home. He also built his own wheelbarrow the shape of which was noticed by other villagers and of course in due time he made and sold several of these at a price which was far less than those in the shops.

This pleasant little wayside corner of Clippesby flourished into a fine garden, producing vegetables and flowers of all varieties. He spent many happy hours busying himself and more often than not with me getting in his way, but he always answered my many and varied questions with never a hint of annoyance at my enthusiasm and yearning to know more and more. Succulent garden peas, beans, sprouts, cabbages and early potatoes were grown to perfection and what an enterprising old gentleman he was! The surplus produce with bundles of flowers were placed on show outside the old chapel house and sold for just a few pence.

Such was the great contrast of yesteryear and today's values, that never once was this little garden vandalised or interfered with; perhaps just a couple of pods of peas disappeared, but nothing else. The only security needed was wire netting compassing the whole plot to keep out the rabbits, and a scarecrow to frighten off the pigeons and other birds, and would you believe this? – it was made in such a way that the head and arms moved even in a slight current of wind and as the old saying goes in Norfolk parlance, 'It dint half put the wind up us, let alone the old badds.'

However, the gypsies were unable to camp there any more, much to our relief, not having to walk that extra distance to school. Time has passed by so quickly and I suppose it is roughly about 55 years since this little garden died and was given back to nature to take its toll, and once more it is now overgrown and very much smaller, but traces of the well can still be defined. The old chapel is in keeping with its departing because only part of the chimney stack remains of its long-ago usefulness. Isn't life sometimes utterly despairing? However, I have photographs to remind me what a snazzy little joint this was.

If you do not like this true account of long ago, please do not remonstrate with me, but place all the blame on my daughter Sandra, because when together we last passed through the Loke I stopped the car and poured out my nostalgic memories and she said, 'Dad, that will make a nice story for the News and Views,' and so again as they utter in Norfolk, 'Here it be!

One of Clippesby's Sons of Repute

I remember back in the 1950s when visiting my family I would often hear and see a Tiger Moth plane circling over the village, and later watch it land on a makeshift runway laid down on the marshes between the village and river. Looking over the marshes from my bedroom window I could also see an aircraft hangar in which the aircraft was housed, serviced and kept up to flying efficiency. The pilot and owner of this plane, as no doubt you have already guessed, was none other than Hugh Showell of Clippesby Hall who later moved down Hall Road a short distance and set up in business as a fruit grower.

Aircraft hangar, now demolished

Not only did Mr Showell watch over and service his plane, he was also a qualified engineer and flew with the Norfolk and Norwich Aero Club and previously was a flying instructor in the R.A.F. during the Second World War. He had flown previously to Spain, North Africa, Tripoli and Italy. Also during June of 1953 and accompanied by a Mr K. Waldron of Ludham he flew to France and they were seventh among 42 entrants in an International air rally. He also worshipped at St Peter's Church where for many years he was Church Warden and sat on various committees in the area of the Fleggs.

However, on Monday, 28th Sept. 1953 it was announced that two days later Hugh was to begin a 12,000 mile voyage to Western Australia, not by sea but by air and not in an air liner, which would take him there in a few days, but on his own in his Auster Aiglet plane. He had by this time changed from the Tiger Moth and he planned to reach Perth in 24 days. For some time Hugh found it was hard work coping with the many formalities which surrounded anyone contemplating a trip such as this one. Sorting out the many papers and documents necessary for a flight such as this he was continuously in the hangar 'tuning' up the Auster and as he said at the time, 'This is not a pleasure trip but solely for business,' and although flying was his main hobby there was a distinct element of adventure about it, no record attempt or anything like that. Nevertheless he believed his would be the first Auster to attempt this long flight, which would take him out of England as autumn approached and into an Australian summer.

He had immersed himself among the many papers and documents he had to take with him, which varied from a certificate of air worthiness to a freight manifest and a licence to operate a small radio - this would be a radio-telephone which would operate within a fifty mile range, also many conversion tables. He suffered a hectic period during which he had often been to London to secure the visas he needed, to Cambridge for his yellow fever inoculation and to other places to arrange other matters.

At his many stops, for example, there must be petrol, and a petrol company had undertaken to see that this would be available at all his planned landing places, even if they had to lump it on the backs of donkeys. The silver and blue aircraft, which replaced his Tiger Moth, would carry sixty-two gallons of fuel, and to make room and space for extra petrol and everything else he had to carry, the back seats were removed. The Auster had a range of 800 miles and a cruising speed of 100 miles per hour.

Among the many items he had to carry were a Very pistol for signalling, a fire extinguisher, survival equipment including a raft, life jacket, emergency rations, medical supplies and the usual paraphernalia useful in the event of a forced landing, health certificates, spares and many other essentials.

He left Southend on Wednesday, 30th Sept. 1953 on the first stage of his journey. At Baghdad (fortunately long before the infamous reign of

91

Saddam Hussein) the Auster would be subject to a fifty-hour inspection, then on to Penang where there would be a hundred-hour inspection. Hugh would be making his third visit to down under, having previously been twice by sea.

B.O.A.C. had arranged accommodation and hangarage for him on this long flight and he hoped he would reach Perth on or about 24th October 1953. He had provisionally arranged to begin his return flight on 16th Dec. 1953, but said he might change his mind about this date.

What a son of this small village of Clippesby he turned out to be and how every parishioner must have been proud of his flight and achievements when he was safely back in their midst, the little Auster aircraft once again in the hangar on the Clippesby marshes. I wonder with what joy and thankfulness they rushed out and glanced skywards as the pulsating drone of the small engine passed overhead to return to its home haven.

We all know that during 1926 the veteran long-distance pilot Alan Cobham flew a De Havilland biplane to Australia and back in 58 days and again in 1930 Amy Johnson at the age of 27 years was the first woman to fly from Britain to Australia solo and again Jim Mollison also accomplished the same feat after which of course there was the romance of the 1930s and finally a splicing of wings. We all knew of course that the exploits of these pilots were made nationally known but our Clippesby pilot was not a man to bask in glory and little was heard of what he did, and without any undue fuss and bother he returned to his fruit-farming venture.

Hugh finished with apples and fruit in the early 1980s and left the shores of the River Bure, dykes and marshes, for the more sunny climes of South Africa but without doubt his nostalgic thoughts are forever within a small hangar on the Clippesby marshes.

My sincere thanks to Mrs Henry Laxon, once a resident of both Clippesby and Fleggburgh for the information and data without which this story would not have been written.

View of the hangar from the top road

Our Scout Troop

Again in the late 1920s whilst Mrs Violet Dyball, a schoolteacher, organised and ran the Girl Guides, Mr Frank Drake was the Scout Master. He was a kind, efficient gentleman who owned and ran the local garage and petrol pumps. Mrs Drake ran the shop where we would spend our pennies and halfpence on sweets etc., before school. The scouts also staged concerts where at the school the partitions would be folded back and we would play to a packed appreciative audience.

On our scout nights, after school I would walk home to Clippesby and, following tea, return to Fleggburgh and then back again after bugle and drum practice and other scout duties. We were taught to be helpful and kind and to salute all prominent persons and those with any standing in society. At the time I did not rightly grasp the meaning of the situation and subsequently saluted almost everything that moved.

Looking back I feel sure our band was enjoyed by every one of the village population, and on Armistice Sunday we would be on parade and sound the 'Last Post' and 'Arouse' at the War Memorial. On other high days and holidays we would march and give displays on the recreation ground. I was the only member from Clippesby and I am positive the local residents were pleased about that, because after practice I would blow my bugle all the way home, and in retrospect I offer my sincere apologies. During the dark winter nights it was more of an act of bravado than anything else, because I was scared to death walking home alone, especially past the farms and through the Loke with its multitude of various noises.

Again on a Saturday morning I would practise from my open bedroom window, giving all Clippesby and Billockby a rousing half hour. Mrs B. Prime of Fleggburgh (Aunt Beatie) will vouch for this – just mention it to her and she will probably burst into uncontrollable hysterics.

I also well remember the Scout Jamboree held at Salhouse and again we walked all the way there and back, pushing our loaded chuck waggon, but what a glorious weekend we all had, meeting other scouts from all over Britain and abroad! The roaring, sparkling and spitting bonfires around which we sat and sang into the late evening before retiring to our tents still flicker across my mind.

Still, my bugle, which must have shattered the reverie of many poor souls, stood me in good stead, because after enlisting into 2nd Bn. Norfolk

93

regiment in 1935 as a drummer and bugler I was quickly on the roster as a regimental guard bugler and later sounded 'Royal Salute', 'General Salute' etc., for Royal families and V.I.P.s for whom the guard would be turned out.

From the recent events occurring in Gibraltar, it brings to mind, whilst we were stationed there between 1937 and 1939, that the guard-room was just across the narrow street adjacent to Government House. After sounding 'Reveille' it was the duty of the bugler to raise the huge Union Jack flag to flutter over the house up to early evening, when 'Retreat' would be sounded, after which he would lower it until the next day. At least three or four times during our week-long guard the governor would turn out the guard and I would sound 'Royal Salute', coming into close contact with many foreign Royals and V.I.P.s, and also many British dignitaries. One of my main nightmares whilst sounding 'Royal Salute', 'Retreat' or 'Last Post' with perhaps hundreds of tourists watching, was to hit a wrong note, but thanks to Mr Drake, never once did this embarrass me.

There is at present a Scout group in Fleggburgh, and may I be permitted to wish them well. It is a worthy cause and commitment, giving joy and great fun and setting a straight path for the future.

94

THE DELINQUENTS

The Delinquents, and Much More

In the early 1920s they said, as it is still said today, that schooldays are the best days of one's life. This probably means during the summer months, and although it may well be so today, it certainly was not so for us during the winter-time of our schooldays.

From Clippesby and Billockby we had to walk to Fleggburgh School and for a youngster from five years old upwards this was a long, long way. We had no coach, taxi or car to pick us up. If it was raining when we left home in the morning our clothes got wet and regardless of how saturated we got we were compelled to remain so all day. It takes little to understand why so many of my generation suffer from acute rheumatism and other disorders of like nature, laughingly referred to as 'rheumatics and lumbergo'.

At play-time, again, everyone had to get out into the playground whatever the state of the weather, and the old pumproom where the ink powder was mixed up and inkwells filled, would only hold about four of us, a tight squeeze at that.

We from the bottom end of the village would wend our way along the main road, whilst those like John Drake, Vina and Nellie Fuller from the top would use Sandy Lane and we would all meet up near the old Police House, where the Chapmans have resided for a number of years. They did, however, take advantage of the footpath which runs across the field from Hall Lane to the road running down to Billockby Church and Hall Farm.

Unable to return home for lunch, packed sandwiches were taken, and during really inclement weather we would be allowed to eat these sitting near the classroom fire, but the weather would have to be extremely severe before this pleasure was allowed. During most of the winter days we were sitting in our wet clothes all day, and although there were coal fires in all four classrooms, presumably to heat the entire room, our teacher had her desk situated slap bang in front of it and very little heat reached out to the class.

When the snow and ice was covering the ground, we had great fun, and it seemed to last for weeks at a time. We could always keep running about and throwing snowballs, and also sliding on the road outside the school gate. Our slides were very short-lived, however; some of them, 20' to 30' in length would soon be covered over with silt from the roadman's shovel.

Our teachers at the time, Mrs Bracey and Mrs Dyball, both cycled from Martham and returned each day, and the headmaster, Mr F. W. Tweddell, did a similar journey from Great Yarmouth. One Friday it snowed nearly all afternoon, and another lad, 'Ickiley' Howes, and myself hatched up a plot to wait outside the school gate after school and pelt the headmaster with snowballs as he left for home. Never once did we think of the consequences involved, and the ultimate conclusion of this stupid escapade. In those days it was ultra-outrageous conduct to besmirch the dignity of the head, but we were young devils and we had also reasoned that being a Friday he had all the weekend to forget the barrage we were to bestow upon him. Oh, how wrong our reasoning was! We had made up several snowballs and when he rode out of the school gate, wham! What a barrage! Although he was hit many times he did not stop or get off his cycle.

On the Monday morning each class lined up as customary outside their respective classrooms before marching in, but once inside school, the partitions were folded back and the full assembly was at hand. I remember being extremely fidgety and uncomfortable when all the teachers came in, followed by the headmaster, who laid the dreaded cane across a desk in full view of everyone. Brief and to the point, he lectured the assembly on the Friday night's occurrence, after which he uttered the dreaded words, 'Howes and Leggett, come out!' I forget which order it was but there was no mistaking the names. Six strokes of the cane, three on each hand. At the first stroke I pulled my hand away and the cane smacked into his leg – I wasn't brave any more. I duly received my punishment and went back to my seat, and young 'Ickiley' received the same.

Unfortunately whilst receiving my punishment on the right hand the cane had struck my thumb, and consequently I could not hold my pen to write. I could do no written lessons that day; in consequence I was given 200 lines, and had to stay in school ten minutes after school each day until completed, starting on the next day, Tuesday. I thought this was most unfair.

During the first playtime session we were the centre of attraction, showing off the already dark blue weals across our palms and fingers, and there were loud 'Cors' all round. However there was no animosity shown towards the headmaster from us, but later on during the afternoon I excused myself from class, went round the back to the cycle shed and kicked his bike. Justice was done, and this more or less evened things up.

In those days the cane was very much in evidence, and I will admit I had more than my fair share, but in retrospect I cannot say it did me any real or lasting harm, only painful memories. Never again, though, was it because of the heinous offence of snowballing our headmaster.

When we set Fire to the Loke

The weeks leading up to firework night were busy and industrious times for all of us in the 1920s. The small amount of pocket or sweet money we managed to squeeze from our parents was used to buy fireworks. During this period there were no restrictions on children and young people going into the shops by themselves and poring over the various types on sale, but in fact there were not very many to choose from; only Catherine wheels, Roman candles, rockets, jumping jacks, squibs and little demons. They were mostly an old ½d or 1d each, and I know that most of the boys, including myself, favoured the ½d little demon which when thrown along someone's garden path or near the back door would cause a terrific explosive bang. With the resultant noise they caused when let off wasn't it only natural they were our firm favourites?

We would form small gangs of two or three and with the collective potential of about three shillings to spend, over a short period of time we would be the proud possessors of 72 noisome and ear-shattering explosions, and for one night of the year we would be allowed out of doors for just perhaps a half-hour later, or perhaps if it was a Saturday or Sunday following, just a little later than that.

This was also the era when acetylene lamps were used on motor cycles and bicycles; the calcium carbide, when in contact with water, would form a gas whilst in a confined space. When our supply of bangers had been exhausted, we resorted to one or two pieces of carbide in an empty treacle or cocoa tin, a small amount of water, the lid jammed on tightly, and a few seconds later, WHAM! – just another way of making a noise. We also used any old bottles we could acquire. With carbide placed inside with a little water, and having been corked up tightly, these would far surpass the noise which erupts when a champagne cork is popped. These really woke up the neighbourhood and the dogs – well, they just barked their heads off.

I would end my night of boyish activity by gazing out of my bedroom window across the marshes, and in line with the river and a wide panorama from Acle to Ludham and further afield, would watch the darkness being lit up with rockets soaring into the sky, terminating in a cascade of glittering profusion, the fire flashes and accompanying bangs, before the sandman made his silent entry and sleep would overcome the most-ever-wanting-to-stay-wide-awake little boy! So another firework night had 'gone and went' as we used to say, consuming with it the impatience and expectancy of waiting. It was now just another night of the past to be quickly forgotten in the sight of oncoming events.

I well remember one Saturday in November or early December, not long after fireworks night, when I was playing with George Cooper (Jewson) and we decided to bake some potatoes. Our fire would be of sticks and wood, in a ditch alongside a field in the Loke. Those readers of Clippesby and Billockby recognise the Loke as a by-road which links the two parishes and forms the base of a triangle, with the top and bottom roads from its apex at Billockby corner. During this time the Loke was bordered by a meadow and a tall thick hedge on one side, with an open field on the other with a ditch on the field side, also surmounted by a bank and hedge. It was the custom of those days for the Council roadman to cut a hole or gap through the roadside bank to the adjacent ditch (holl) to allow water to run off the road and one such hole was the ideal spot for our fire – or so we thought!

Everything was going fine as we piled sticks and wood on with our potatoes underneath, but we had not envisaged or contemplated the unpredictable effect of a light breeze. Now, of course you are all well ahead of me, and your suppositions are justifiably founded, because we did, in fact, set fire to the Loke, and when the hedge really started to blaze and the smoke billowed skywards, I'll give anything to wager you would have done the exact same thing as we did; you wouldn't? – well we did, as fast as our legs would get us out of there and into hiding in the plantation at Billockby corner, frightened beyond talking point, staring at each other with disbelieving wide open eyes.

Fortunately for us both, no damage was caused other than one hedge being completely burnt down.

On arriving home for tea, I suppose my uncertain sheepish grin gave me away and there were the usual questions of where have you been?– did you? – was I? – had I? – to all of which I just said 'No', and shook my head.

Come on now, wouldn't you all do the same? Nevertheless, and in spite of my protestations, I had to submit to another good hiding and the inevitable climb up the wooden hill to bed. How was I to know that exuding above the natural country schoolboy pong, I smelt like a heap of burning rubbish where the smoke had embraced my clothes?

Years later when in the Army and during my spells at home on leave, 'Jewson' and I would partake of a drink or two and he would unfailingly toast my home-coming, 'Just to quench and put out the Loke fire!'

Happy days!

Billockby Corner

As a small boy during the 1920s, I remember one of the favourite spots occupied by some of the young and indeed the older residents of the two close-knit parishes of Billockby and Clippesby during late spring and into summer, and that was at the corner, locally referred to as Billockby Corner, with the plantation standing in Clippesby as its background. Some folks will doubtless still remember the triangular raised piece of grassed area, which had most probably been there from the time when, from Acle along the turnpike, the roads through the two villages had been nothing more than overgrown dirt tracks. This small piece of land was an island, sporting firstly a wooden, and later on a wrought iron finger direction post, directing travellers to Martham and Potter Heigham, or Filby and Caister-on-Sea. The old stone cottage which stood at the dividing point was at the time the home of an old lady, Mrs Siely, and George and Mrs Abel and their two sons, Ted and Geoffrey. Geoffrey was one of my school and 'getting-into-trouble-and-mischief' friends.

On a Sunday afternoon several would gather on this little island and watch, as cyclists, tandem riders, motorcycle combinations with four or five-up would pass by in their hundreds, en route for the sea and beach and Hemsby, Caister and Great Yarmouth, having travelled from Norwich. Scores of the old baby Austins and bull-nosed Morris cars with their spoked wheels would trundle past. Ownership of this type of transport was made possible by the then on-the-crest-of-a-wave affluent boot and shoe industry in Norwich, where wages at this time were probably three times that of the agricultural worker.

100

From an early age I had been taught by my brother Freddie how to repair punctures and a broken chain, and it was not very long before I became aware of the lucrative possibilities which could be on offer from the pedal cyclists, some of whom had no idea whatsoever how to repair a puncture. I therefore equipped myself with a cycle pump, scissors, an old rubber cycle tube for patches, rubber solution, some rough-striking matchboxes and three old spoons to remove the tyres, and although this emptied my red-post-office tin money box and I was sorely financially broke, I had great hopes of it rattling from within long before the next Sunday School outing.

I suppose some of you will still recall the old milestone which was positioned along the causeway, stating that Norwich was 13 miles and Great Yarmouth 9 miles – well, against this milestone I placed my little notice, 'PUNCTURES MENDED 1/-'. And I was doing very well indeed, anything from 5/- to 10/- for a Sunday afternoon when men working on the farms were only earning 30/- per week. Punctures were fairly frequent and my savings grew until my mother suddenly tumbled to the fact that my pockets were getting torn and holey through carrying old and discarded boot hobnails and studs in addition to a few tacks, a lot of which she found. Of course she told my father and between them two and two were added together to make five and so on, after which my father took off his leather belt and I knew then what people meant when they uttered, 'Ent life sicknen'.'

From then on I was with the others on the grass island. One or two punctures came my way but with such infrequency it was downright disheartening, but nevertheless we all enjoyed ourselves watching the people passing by.

Also at this time the 'gret ole sharrabangs' had started their weekend runs to the coast, and these lumbered and rumbled past on their solid-tyred wheels, but with happy and smiling people out for the day laughing and singing all the way.

These vehicles were always gaily painted and each one had a name in running script on the rear, such as 'Primrose', 'Caroline', 'Daffodil' and many more. They were open to the elements but a canvas hooded cover which folded up and over from the rear to the front windscreen would quickly be assembled if the rains came.

Normally on a Sunday morning whilst in season, a hawker with a horse and cart would visit all the surrounding villages selling crabs, winkles and

101

shrimps, ringing a hand bell to alert people to his whereabouts, and later, between the hours of four and five in the afternoon, everyone would be taking tea of the luscious and succulent shellfish. On some Sundays perhaps a tin of salmon would be opened as a special treat, but I remember always there was a large glass bowl of trifle with custard and jellies.

At the stone cottages on the corner was the recognised bus stop when buses started to run from Norwich to Great Yarmouth and back, and those people from the top of Clippesby, Thurne, Oby and the outlying villages would cycle to the corner and leave their bikes in Mrs Abel's garden. Later on, when the buses took on the carrying of parcels and other small goods, agents were appointed to receive and deliver these items and Mrs Abel became one of these agents. She would deliver those to addresses in the near vicinity but those living further afield would have to collect, and I suppose that at this period the small amount of money which she earned from this project helped with the house-keeping.

This system lasted for several years but later, after the war, the service was discontinued, and as motor cars and other vehicles became faster and faster, the finger-post directional sign was knocked down and broken and the offending vehicle would often end up through the small garden fence and into the front of the house. These occasions became more and more frequent and especially uncomfortable to the occupants, as vehicles again became faster, and not only did the trustworthy old post keep getting demolished and the garden fence torn and tattered, but the corner wall of the cottage was continually being struck and large holes appeared, the impacts causing serious wall damage and severe disturbance to the foundations. In time it was said by the 'elected persons in high positions', 'Who put that grass patch and sign post in such a stupid place in the road?' Also, 'What idiot ever dreamed of building a house at a Y junction and bend in the road to hamper and impede our beloved motor vehicles so that they cannot take the corner properly at high speed?'

Everybody in the two parishes can now see the outcome; the old stone cottage has disappeared, being so badly damaged when a lorry ran into it that it had to be demolished. There now stands in its place a new and more modern semi-detached dwelling, but a wee bit further back from the road. But in the distant future as vehicles are manufactured to move faster and faster, and are driven more inconsiderately, will this, too, suffer the same fate?

On wet and horrible winter mornings we children were given one (old) penny for our bus fare to Fleggburgh School and I remember standing with the others against the black tarred wall of the old cottage, gazing along the turnpike towards Acle waiting to see the first glimpse of the jolly old bus to show up in the distance, when someone would suggest we run to school and thereby save our bus fare to buy sweets, and two or three of us would do this. We found that by running the distance between three telegraph poles and walking between one, we could reach the gates of the school more or less at the same time as the bus.

One of the other enjoyable highlights of our little lives some afternoons was the arrival of the man on the tricycle bearing the sign 'STOP ME AND BUY ONE'. Wall's ice cream had come up with the splendid idea of a man pedalling a tricycle, the front of which was a large box container about three feet square, from which was sold ice cream, old-type iced lollies, and the most of all sought-after 'Snofruit', which was in triangular shape and just frozen fruit juice, but how we loved them at one (old) penny each! I'll guarantee that the mere mention of these small luxuries will again enhance the taste buds of those who still remember them.

However, this was in the time of around 1926/7, and I'm thinking now what Billockby Corner will be and look like in 2027. Will a house still be standing there at its junction, or will part of a new motorway be running over its foundations? And not forgetting the old plantation, the haven of my school days, where we climbed the trees, gathered nuts and pussy willow, pinched birds' eggs, etc. – will this just be a blob on an ancient map?

The Fag-end Roll-ups.

In this day and age smoking is gradually becoming a pleasure of the past. I say pleasure because those who did smoke, whether it be pipe, cigar or cigarette, arose from their slumbers each morning with a furred tongue, unsavoury and not unlike the coconut matting on the outside doorstep and a mouth with sympathetic consideration for the bottom of a ferret box, and breath so vile the dog turned away from his good morning greeting. The hacking fits of coughing were heard all over the neighbourhood and when several were at it the valley of echoes was put to shame and a very poor second.

I honestly remember people saying, when they lit up their first cigarette to start off the day and whilst supping the first cuppa, 'thar's nuthen like a good ole corf ta git them there lungs a-warken'.'

I remember the briar and other pipes of all shapes and sizes, especially the long stemmed white clay pipes but most of all the awful black pungent smoke which was emitted from mouth and nose, 'a-cleren out the ole neersels' they would say, and all made possible from the blackish coloured tobacco which was named Churchman's Counter Shag.

The majority of smokers suffered year after year with bad chests, and bronchitis was chronic with the addition of allied complaints and the wheezing, fighting-for-breath adult was commonplace in every community. Not only did they smoke but it was also chewed as well, 'chowed' was the description given to it and a lump the size of a filbert nut was chewed like gum with the tell-tale brown streaks dripping down from the corners of the mouth and running down the chin but not until the spit, which was constant, lost its brown texture was it discarded; revolting but all so very true. The chew itself was called a 'chow' or 'wad' and 'verra good fer tutheark' they said.

I cannot remember any man who did not indulge in the art of puffing but it is fair to say that in my young days I knew not of any woman that did, but they certainly made up for lost decades when the war started and have carried on ever since with a vengeance.

At schoolboy age all would imitate their elders and consequently short ends were picked up, a packet of fag papers bought from the shop for 1d. and, as the saying went, 'we rolled our own' but always keeping a sharp weather eye open for the policeman; smoking was not allowed by law until one was 15 years of age and a boy would constantly speak of the day when he would attain this age and become manly.

I well remember I went to school with one Gordon Woolston, whose family was a large one and in those days were scraping the earth to survive, but when Gordon left school he worked on a farm for a Mr Jeffries at Hall Farm, Billockby, for a wage of 10s. per week. In those days a mother held the purse strings and his dear old Mum bought for him a packet of 20 Kensitas brand of cigarettes every day at a cost of 11½d. per packet, just over 8s. 4d. per week, leaving just 1s. 6d. (7p) from his total wages. But then each packet contained a card and a consolation free gift voucher and the family were overjoyed to choose the free gifts available and their shelves and sideboard were adorned with numerous little ornaments and useless items.

So far, you have in your minds and will be thinking, 'what a tedious old boy he is this month,' but no, I was only leading up to the more 'pleasant' side of weed addiction, that being the occupational effort and time spent in collecting cigarette cards. There were many tobacco companies who produced various brands of smokes and each and every packet contained a picturesque card which not all, but most, schoolboys collected. I have two albums, one of which is marked with my name and address bearing the date 1927, and another 1928, containing sets of 50 and sometimes 100 cards such as Birds and Animals, Football, Rugby and Cricket Players, Boxers, Old Naval and Army Uniforms, Filmstars and Notables, Fortune-telling, Medals, Dogs, Sportsmen, Flags of all Nations, Military Headwear and Old Fire Engines etc. What a dextrous little devil I was in those days as those cards were mostly obtained by asking, 'Heyya gotta fag card, Mister.' Reggie Key at South Farm, Clippesby, was one of my greatest sources as I would always be in his shadow pottering around the farm with him and I would run down to Hudson's shop with a 6d. for his packet of 10 Players Navy Cut. Naturally, in keeping with others and having acquired the habit, I smoked a few cigarettes but a great many more when I went into the Army, and to my shame, many, many, more when abroad and in the confines of the W.O.s' and Sgts' Mess, where they were freely obtainable.

However, I stopped in 1952, and after much anguish and the gnawing pains of withdrawal, I have never indulged to this day, and since that date I have always felt a much fitter, healthier and cleaner person. I breathe easily and have no cough, my mouth and tongue feels sweet and fresh. I am also overjoyed to know that my son and two daughters are abstainers, but from

July 30th 1982, I have retained two packets of cigarettes, still enclosed in the original cellophane wrapping as a grim reminder of the tragedy which the 'pleasure' I described in my opening paragraph can cause by destroying one of a happy family group. Both packets lay in a large ashtray in my front room and when my visitors become inquisitive I tell them a sad story, and I often think to myself, 'so much for my beautiful sets of cigarette cards.'

The Wasps

Again in the late 1920s, from the second week in July, fruit picking at Tooke's Farm would be in full operation. This farm is down the narrow track off Sandy Lane, just a short distance from the main Fleggburgh road. Nearly all the ladies of the villages would pick fruit and as the children came out of school we would locate our respective parent along the rows of tall raspberry canes and assist in the picking. The hard-earned money would supplement the family needs and other expenses.

At the finish of the day the ladies from Clippesby and Billockby would walk home by way of Sandy Lane on to the Clippesby road, and I well remember how regularly every year, wasps would have a nest in the bank at the bend in the road, just prior to South House Farm.

I can tell you now, there is nothing more infuriating to a nest of wasps than to have a long stick poked down into the nest and waggled about. A thorough good poking would render them mad enough to attack anything or anyone passing by. I waited until the ladies were in near proximity and then did my deed and took to my heels like the wind. Oh, boy! were those wasps upset! They were real mean and angry.

From my safe spot in the farm yard I can still remember to this day the stampede down the hill towards the farm, baskets of fruit held high and skirts up above the knees; it must have certainly cured the aches and pains of the day's toil. My self-acquired complacency, however, was short-lived, because as is usual somebody told tales, and as I walked indoors I was met by Mother covered in blue from blue bags and wielding a cane. I spent the rest of the day and evening hungry and gazing over the marshes from my bedroom window. Still, I didn't mind too much; I had eaten plenty of raspberries.

The next evening my mother was sewing away when she delivered her lecture on me. My father sat smoking his pipe at one side of the fireplace, my grandfather at the other, and I noticed that my father coughed once or twice and there was a sheepish grin on the face of my grandfather. I was too young then to realise and understand that this boyish prank had been played before, many years before, and there was nothing new about it. Kids had poked at wasps' nests and received chastisement for doing so down through the ages. The only newness about this episode was my aching bottom.

Meantime, around the countryside the hedges, ditches and banks had been trimmed and cut, the feeling of harvest was in the air, and we were eagerly awaiting our last day at school before breaking up for the summer holidays at the end of July.

None of us could wait; we were all agog and awaiting the chasing of rabbits in the harvest fields, and enjoying the sun and fine weather to come, and, yes, it did seem that in those days, except for the odd thunder and lightning storm, the weather was indeed beautiful and sunny. Before many days had elapsed our little bodies would be brown and dark tanned. School and exams would be forgotten and in the past, for the time being.

'I remember, I remember...'

About 1929-30 only 'grown-ups' possessed bikes, but I acquired my first bike at quite an early age and everyone in the village predicted I would break my neck, and indeed, I must admit I did my worst to prove them right.

I found a lady's cycle frame, the sit-up-and-beg type, which someone had dumped, and I fitted to this two large old-fashioned pram wheels (minus the solid rubber tyres), handlebars, and, to the top of the seat stem, a cushion tied with 'binder twine'. I was then in business. Did I hear someone mention brakes?

On the straight I would have to 'hobby horse' walk uphill, and go a blinder downhill. On the hill going down towards South House and the farm, I would get up a good speed and, of course, having no tyres on the wheels the sparks would fly out from behind, and when in full flight I must have resembled a miniature meteor. Sparks would also fly off my hobnailed boots (my brakes). Many times I would come to grief if a vehicle did happen to approach me, or I skidded, and I would end up in the ditch, or 'holl', at the side of the road near the cow shed. If the opportunity arose I would make an emergency broadside into the farmyard in a cloud of dust.

Reggie Key will probably still remember this futuristic contraption, for at the time his father Jack Key owned the farm, and it was about the same time when Reggie bought his first Bedford lorry/cattle float. He will also doubtless remember how Bertie Woods and myself almost got to blows over the Players cigarette cards after one or both of us had gone down to the village shop to get a packet of ten Players cigarettes for an old 6d. Did I hear someone say, shop? Yes, we did once have a shop, which was owned and run by Mrs Hudson. Her husband, Sam, a retired Liverpool policeman, would spend his time sitting outside in the shade of an oak tree, whilst continuously smoking a pipe. He was often accompanied by Mr George Abel, who lived near the plantation at Billockby corner in the house which was demolished, and where there now stands a new semi-detached, wisely at a greater distance from the 'road hogs'.

At this period, our parson was the Rev. Owen Manby, living at Clippesby Rectory. He was of small stature, always dressed in sombre black, and wore a black trilby. He always carried a black umbrella and almost every Saturday morning he could be seen walking down the middle of the road, twirling the umbrella round and round and intent on going either to Norwich or Great Yarmouth. I say 'either', because it depended from which direction the first car came. On reaching the main road at Billockby Corner he would position himself in the middle of the road and at the first sighting of any vehicle he would start to jump up and down whilst waving his umbrella madly, and the surprised driver would be compelled to stop and offer him a lift.

Because Sam Hudson was always outside the shop, the reverend gentleman would leave his big black coat hanging from the oak tree, near the shop (a very early security service) for safe custody. One Saturday morning a rat was killed on the road near the Loke (now referred to as 'By Road') and I waited until Sam had gone to his dinner, and, holding the dead rat by the tail, slipped it into the coat pocket. Whether I was seen doing this I do not rightly know, but subsequently there was a considerable amount of laughable comment going round the village, and later on I was singled out to take the blame. More credit was also given to me because shortly after this I joined the choir of Fleggburgh church and in view of this could not also attend at Clippesby. Fleggburgh boasted a good choir of about twenty – does anyone remember Ike Carter? Another incentive for joining the choir was the 2/6d we were paid each quarter. For a young and small lad it was quite a walk from Clippesby to Fleggburgh and back each Sunday evening. Choir practice was also held once every week, and this meant an extra journey during the early evening.

The Rev. Manby christened me as a baby and I have often wondered if he may have been sorely tempted to bend the rules a wee bit if he could have just glimpsed into the future. The coat was never left there again, and a good thing really, because with my boyish enthusiasm the poor man would probably have ended up with a collection of birds, mice, and, who knows, I believe he knew I was the culprit because prior to the incident he would often refer to me as 'James', but afterwards it was, 'Hello, young man!'

Deep down, though, I knew I was forgiven.

Fleggburgh Church

Hoops & Things

Unfortunately during the late 1920s we did not enjoy the toys and pocket money, or the lavish trappings bestowed on the children of today. Our amusements, sports and day to day enjoyments were devised and put to test by our own efforts alone. We had seasons of various activities which included, hoops, tops, tip-pit, conkers, marbles, bird-nesting, etc., whilst the girls would play hopscotch, various ball games and the inevitable skipping ropes which would twirl and whir. I can still hear the incessant chants of '1-2-3 Oh! Learey', and 'salt-pepper-vinegar'.

Our hoop outfit would consist of a spoked cycle wheel with the spokes and hub removed and a nut stick cut from the plantation. The stick held vertically inside the rim would propel the hoop along, creating a beautiful, intensely noisy rattle on the road surface. Unfortunately hoops were banned from the school precincts and we lads from Clippesby and Billockby were somewhat at a loss as to where to leave our precious 'Rolls Royces' of the day whilst at school.

However, Horney Osborne from the top road, over the weekend, called for a meeting, which included the persons of Geoffrey Abel, Billy Hunn, Herbert (Quilt) Cooper, Harry Woolston, Bertie Woods and myself, and it was decided we should have a garage to deter any despicable and nasty intentions from would-be vandals. Oh yes, hoop thieves were about even in those days! We had one heck of an argument as to the location of our site, so a committee was formed and, as still so happens today, we decided not to agree and Horney Osborne took over complete control, and became our leader. Eventually a property was acquired in a dry ditch by the side of the road and secluded by a thick hedge, just past the entrance to Sandy Lane and adjacent to the Council dump which still survives.

On the Monday morning we assembled at the top of the Loke on the Billockby main road and with panache started off running abreast along the road. On passing Hall Farm the dogs barked madly and we must have resembled the epic Chariot race in 'Ben Hur' for such was our exuberance as our tyreless hoops resounded against the hard metal of the road, and again, what a spectacle we must have portrayed as we rounded the left hand bend in the road at High House Farm, and on along the road past the Police House (now Chapman's) and then, through a gap in the hedge, we reached our garage. There, secluded from prying eyes and nailed to a wood batten was a cardboard sign: 'HOP GARAGE'.

Constantly our teachers were reminding us of the fact that put together our brightness would not illuminate the candles on a Christmas tree, but hold you hard, the more learned amongst us spotted at once that Horney had created a misnomer; he had obviously lost a h(o)op from the word HOOP. Was this a deliberate mistake, a ruse or something more sinister to start the first fight of the day? But we proved our teachers wrong in that we sought diplomacy to solve this awkward problem in this instance: you see, Horney was bigger than we were – that's why he became our self-appointed leader. I believe it was Abraham Lincoln who once said, 'Diplomacy is the blood brother of hypocrisy.'

Incidentally our garage site is still existent today, after all the years have passed, and only last Easter I pointed it out to Sandra and Denise as we were passing on our way to Fleggburgh.

Also the story is absolutely true.

The Rabbit-skin Tickets

During my schooldays in the 1920s I recall that at any time during the day or night, rabbits abounded in all parts of the countryside. There were more of these furry creatures than the farmers and landowners could afford to

111

feed and supply homes to, and around the headlands of cropped fields one could see the evidence of their feeding habits. Banks and hedges were eroded with countless holes and burrows ran underground like miniature labyrinths. This was also the time when the hideous gin traps were set out and staked down in runs; wire snares were suspended in tracks through hedges and banks and sometimes caused agonizing death to other wildlife apart from rabbits. On Saturday afternoons and Sunday mornings, especially during the winter months, one could see small groups of three to four men armed with shotgun, spade and the wily ferret, along the banks and hedgerows and the numbers of rabbits caught would be shared out to eat and the surplus either given or sold to near neighbours. At various markets around the area wild rabbits were sold in hundreds, eventually finding their way on to the dinner plates of those dwelling in towns and cities.

Even though every farmer and landowner moaned and groaned and wrung their hands in desperation as the bobbing white tails flashed their unwelcome presence in the fields, very few of them allowed anyone, not even their own workers, to assist in the problem of decimating the ever-growing numbers. It was not fully or completely understood why this was so as, on the one hand, some were hungry and would be able to eat and the other would see more return from his crops. Even the law had its say and to quote, 'Trespassing on land in pursuit of conies' was the wording on the summons. A court appearance would mean a £2 fine which at the time was more than the wages for a week. Nevertheless large numbers were caught and eaten, the meat being clean and wholesome, the rabbit having fed on the crops and vegetation which nature provided.

As I have mentioned before in other 'I remember' stories, the rabbit skins were hung up to dry on a nail or hook driven into the house wall where they would remain suspended until the 'Look-em-up' man made one of his visits with a horse and cart, heralding his presence with a booming voice of 'Lumbo-Lumbo', and he would buy all lumber such as metals, iron, rags, bones, rabbit and mole skins.

However, at the time when I was about 12 years of age I had put together a 'bitza bike' and had even acquired two bicycle oil lamps, white glass to the front and red to the rear with the appropriate brackets. I could mend a puncture, repair a broken chain and in fact get myself out of any bicycle problems which might arise. I could not afford new cycle tyres and had to be satisfied with those thrown away by the big 'grown ups' and where there was a hole in the tread another piece of tyre was cut up, the wire beading removed and a portion of about four to six inches placed underneath to cover it. A wee bit bumpy but nevertheless a substantial repair job. Also, about this time, there was talk of being able to get in and see the pictures in Norwich by offering two or three rabbit skins in payment for entry and I eyed up the skins on our outside wall as a prospective ticket for me to see a 'Laurel and Hardy'.

On a Saturday morning, having collected four rabbit skins and carrying tools, patches, solution, scissors, spare tyre and tube, bits of chain links and the two oil lamps filled with oil and wicks trimmed, I set off for Norwich some fourteen miles away. With all the do's and don'ts and a packet of sandwiches, my mother saw me off firmly convinced that the sandwiches would be eaten before I even reached Acle and I would be returning home feeling a little subdued – but she was wrong, as this was not to be as she thought. I was not too worried about the tales and talk of Norwich boys setting themselves on strangers to the City as I was a pretty tough handful for my age and could fight like a young tiger.

I rode along steadily and thought I was a real hero when, on reaching the river at Thorpe St Andrew, I stopped and ate my sandwiches under the horse chestnut tree there on the river green. Funny thing isn't it, how repeats seem to come along during one's life span because, when as a respected limb of the law twenty-two years later I was stationed at Thorpe St Andrew, I often sat under the same horse chestnut tree and reminisced, whilst Sandra and Paul played on the river green; incidentally it is still growing there, a magnificent specimen and much larger too.

I eventually arrived at Foundry Bridge in Norwich, opposite the railway station where traffic of the day worried me quite a bit. There were trams clanking along noisily, the drivers ringing their bells and seemingly bearing down on me from all directions, horses drawing carts and wagons, vendors pushing and pulling handcarts. The noise was tremendous but I suppose typical of the City going about its business and I pushed my bike along the pavement till I came to the first cinema in Prince of Wales Road. I secured my bike with the largest linked chain and padlock one could ever set eyes upon and timidly, with trepidation and faltering steps entered the brightly-lit foyer where a man in a colourful uniform sporting a row of medals took my rabbit skins. He led me to a side door and in the darkness a young lady took me down to my seat, right in the very front row where I had to crane

113

my neck to look up at the picture, but I didn't care, I was there, I had made it, and I thought, 'I'll bet my mother is sorry she ever doubted me.'

During the interval when the lights came on I saw the people making their way to a door marked TOILET and, wondering why, I went too and realised what it was – but at home we didn't call ours by that name. I went several times after that, not to really go but just to pull the chain and see the water flush out and I thought, 'Wait till I get home and tell them all about this.' I saw the films round twice and a bit and made my way out, unlocked my bike, pushed it along the pavement until I was over the river bridge whilst being very wary of the trams. I then lit my oil lamps, like the proverbial utterance, saying, 'Home James.' I didn't know what time it was but on passing through Blofield in the darkness I heard a shout, 'Oigh, where do you think you are going?' and I found it to be the village policeman setting up one of the early and first types of speed trap. I didn't know my rear lamp had blown out. He wanted to know everything, as most policemen did, but after a lot of questioning I was allowed to go on. He lit my lamp for me: I explained my mother would not allow me to carry matches, and it was a good thing I was not searched, because he would have found some red-headed matches, three woodbines and several short ends in my pockets. Again, funny how things repeat themselves as I was stationed at Blofield and Brundall before moving to Thorpe St Andrew.

However, on reaching Acle, I knew I was close to home and when about ten minutes later I opened our back door I received an enormous 'ding of the lug', and God only knows what for because it was only just gone ten o'clock and I had only been away for thirteen hours.

I went to the pictures in Norwich roughly five or six times each year, biking the 26 miles there and back, almost up to the time when I left home at the ripe old age of fifteen to seek my fortune. Pulling the chain in the toilet still intrigued me; we still hadn't got those new-fangled contraptions down our way at Clippesby and even the good old, ever-remembered honey-cart wasn't thought of until later.

I still remember the roast rabbit with pork, rabbit and pigeon pie with a covering of delicious crust, and I sometimes rack my thinking capabilities and wonder why we destroyed our rabbit population by using that insidious pox myxomatosis causing great suffering; they never ever deserved degradation such as this and we now import rabbits from China, selling at a very high price.

114

May I also point out the differences in the price of cinema seats – once upon a time three or four rabbit skins and now £3.00 or £4.00 but of course one luxury has not changed, although a bit more modern perhaps; the chain is still there for the pulling. Some folks didn't even know the pleasure of the 'honey-cart' and some, I think, wish they never had.

The House on the Marshes

During the 1920s, on a Saturday night when we were on holiday from school we were never bored with our situation in life and always found something to occupy our agile minds and adventurous thoughts. On the previous two or three last days at school we would talk up and someone would suggest we made our yearly visit to the old house across the marshes and quite near to the river.

It had been, or so we thought, a marshman's cottage but had been abandoned for many years even then and was in a sorry state of dilapidation and sad disrepair; although parts of the roof had disappeared the stairs remained in sufficient strength to enable a climb up to the windows from which we had a commanding vista over the expanse of the marshes along the river towards both Acle and Thurne.

We, that was usually Geoffrey Abel, Billy Hunn, Georgie (Jewson) Cooper and myself, started off carrying our sandwiches and bottles of cold tea which was supposedly for dinner but all had been drunk and consumed usually within the first half hour of leaving home; it was easier to carry on the inside.

As can still be seen from today's observations from the Acle causeway the river is quite some distance across the marshes and although gates were in existence to afford entry for the movement of cattle, why use these when there were dykes to be jumped? Not always did one cross over safely as, when about to jump, one foot would embed itself into the soft muddy bank and so with squishes and squelches and slurpy sounds inevitably a resounding splash would be heard and the unfortunate one would be pulled out covered in duckweed, rotting vegetation and sometimes attached to the legs or arms one or two black 'beasties.'

Once there, this was a most wonderful playground and old apple trees, although gnarled and cankered, produced an abundance of sour green apples of which, although we knew by the very partaking of same we would suffer dreadfully afterwards, we ate our fill and so it was the next day came the sufferance of terrible tummy pains and Mother said, 'that's as good as a dose of syrup of figs' and a lot better than being 'bound up' and having to see Doctor Tom Roydon to get a 'dollop' of the nasty stuff he 'doled out.'

At that time large barges plied their varied trades along the river and we would watch them coming up in the distance and then sit on the river bank to watch them pass by. These barges were the pride and joy of my schooldays and I thought the most graceful craft afloat on the river at this time.

Even the old and secluded small structure down the bottom of the garden was still standing. Admittedly some roof tiles were missing, the door hanging off its hinges, some bricks had fallen from the walls which were crumbling but the door, although worse for want of repairing and several coats of paint, still sported the nail on the inside which held the binder twine, which in turn held the torn-to-about-six-inches squares of newspaper from the daily paper and in easy reach of the sitter. The whole seat structure was still there, festooned with tangled masses of spiders' webs, also plentifully dotted with hundreds of woodworm holes. Although overgrown and somewhat wild, the extremities of the garden could still be defined, with flintstones, wood and oddments denoting the area of the path to the aforementioned privy.

When I think back to those far off days when I saw someone walking down the garden path with newspaper in hand and hoping for a quiet read, only one apparent destination was obvious and a wicked minded little boy would wait until he or she was nicely settled and then bombard the door with apples, if in season, and clods of earth. On occasions the door sneck would be tied with string, the end of which would be anchored to a rabbit's hutch or something similar. Amongst other oddities all boys of my age without fail carried string in our pockets and always that indispensable blade, the 'shut-knife.'

I knew, or thought I knew, I was safe from detection taking in all the immediate circumstances but someone somewhere would see the boy 'Jimma' sneaking out through the garden gate or a gap in the hedge and many were the times I received a 'Gret old ding-a-tha-lug' for my indiscretion. There were always eyes in hiding behind the slightly drawn curtains, altered into inquisitiveness after hearing the lumps and bangs as the clods hit the privy door and the echoing angry shouts or screams following frustrated disruption. I would attend Sunday School and sing in the choir and ask for forgiveness, and I believe it was sometimes granted because I was not always found out and got away with quite a lot.

However, about tea time we would venture back to civilization, probably falling into the dykes again on the way and so, filthy and dirty, dishevelled beyond description and not at all smelling too sweetly, we faced our respective 'Maters.'

Mine was well prepared for my homecoming and the copper stove had always been lit in anticipation with oodles of piping hot water bubbling away inside. Off the nail on the outside wall came the tin bath and a half hour or so later, a once odious little boy was spick and span again, but not for very long; sitting down to a well deserved tea and smelling strongly of carbolic soap. What an exhausting day I had had and I reminisced as I tucked into my roast wild rabbit, three veg. and Yorkshire puddings - not forgetting the gravy.

My Mother remarked to my Father, 'Wot a datty little old warmun he wus wen he cum hoom sarter-nune.'

Grannie would kindly please help in explaining about the little structure along the garden path in which the paper was read, and go on to include the reason for the 'honey-cart.' Thanks!

SPECIAL EVENTS AND COUNTRY GAMES

My Trips to Norwich

During the middle 1920s I can well remember the months of January and February were always cold and wet and mostly miserable. The long walk to school, probably in the rain and remaining in wet clothes all day, and the return home as darkness was falling, rendered all outside activity to a minimum, except for weekends. However, at this time of year I usually made one of my two trips to Norwich with my mother and grandfather (Fred Curson), both of which were beneficial for me. During his working life my grandfather had been occupied as a farm steward, had acted wisely and consequently during his long retirement was fairly comfortable, financially. My visit to the big City would be to fit me out with clothes and boots before each new term at school commenced.

We were usually about early on the day, and following breakfast would set off on foot to Acle railway station. Although this was over two miles distant there was plenty to occupy my mind. The causeway at this time was bordered by dykes on each side with willow trees set at regular close settings of about twelve feet from Billockby Corner up to and over Acle Bridge to the old Hermitage Sun. Each and every one was watched over and maintained by the Council, with no harsh wide gaps and deterioration as there is today, and the effect it gave was of walking down a beautiful avenue in a green and pleasant landscape.

I would be interested in the numerous windmills on the marshes, and was always fascinated by their massive turning sails. St Margaret's Mill, near the Stokesby road, was in use and fully working at this time, and being so close to the road one could see it operating in all its splendid and massive power. Also, with only a few hardy cattle on the marshes at this

time of year, the activities of that little velvet-coated gentleman could be plainly seen and hundreds of mole hills appeared like miniature mud huts dotted around a grassy landscape.

On reaching the station and obtaining our tickets there was always a wait before the train arrived, and as Grandfather knew the Station Master and porters, he would be catching up with local news and talk. The station had well-kept and attractive flower gardens during this period, and with porters' barrows, milk churns, packages of all descriptions, various paraphernalia and even cattle in the station pens, there was enough to hold my attention. The signal arms, moving noisily, announced the approaching train, and with its whistle blowing and belching clouds of steam and smoke it pulled into the station. The porters were busy unloading and again loading articles into the guard's van, and then with a whistle and the wave of a green flag we were away, with bumps and bangs and eventually into the familiar chorus of 'Bibbidy Bee – Bibbidy Bob' as the wheels ran over the rail joints.

Arriving at Thorpe Station, again there was a general bustling activity, the smell of steam and acrid smoke, and then outside in the streets there were horses and carts and men pushing and pulling handcarts and vying for position with the trams clanking and ringing their bells along the varied thoroughfares. We made our way to London Street where at its junction with Castle Street and Swan Lane stood the impressive and ornate building of the London Provincial Bank at which place Grandfather withdrew some of the interest accumulating on his account there. Incidentally this building is still in evidence but is now a bookshop, and as I pass it on many occasions I am brought suddenly to remember how it was in its hey-day. Nostalgia runs rampant sometimes and I flip into another time past and eventually find I have gone a long way before recapturing the present time.

From here we walked the small distance away and along Castle Meadow to Orford Place to the outfitters' huge shop of one Thomas Boston, at which I was totally fitted out, and other items of clothing and footwear were purchased for other members of the family.

Following this, we would have tea and cakes at the renowned 'Princes' eating place near the Guildhall at the corner of Exchange Street, after which we visited the near-by market place where Grandfather would buy an enormous joint of beef, and next door, for young James, an ice-cream cornet. My mother bought several yards of various types of sewing material to make up items of clothing during the forthcoming weeks, when during

121

the evenings she would be sewing away happily. She was a very talented seamstress.

Several other shops were visited in other parts of the City, and then it was time to return to the station and on to Acle and walk home. My goodness, I was tired when I eventually arrived home; we must have walked at least six or seven miles, and on the way home were carrying heavy packages – and, don't forget, I walked a lot further, as I took two steps to one of my grandfather's, and then they wondered why my boots wore out so soon! Still, I was very lucky in some ways as most of the kids in our day had never ridden on a train or seen a Norwich tram.

As I walk round the City centre and reminisce, I sometimes realize that all the shops we visited during my boyhood have long since disappeared and only survive on old photographs; 'progress' is the actual phrase the powers that be use to describe their handiwork.

However, on the funnier side, I met Aunt Beattie Prime at Ken and Mona's farewell party at Rollesby and she said to me, 'You young so and so, you! Do you remember when you poured water into the petrol tank of the school master's motor bike?' How can I not remember, when I still have marks on certain parts of my anatomy to remind me!

The Ancient Game of Quoits

With reference to the above and the account by our friend Mary Cooke, this certainly brought back many memories of my boyhood.

My father was umpire for the Clippesby team, and as a young lad I would watch the play, accompanied by my friend John Drake, whose parents lived in the house now occupied by Bob and Joan Somerville, his father being the farm foreman for Frederick Key, who also farmed at Mundham. The pitch was in a corner of the meadow adjoining the private road to the cottages, woods and marshes just south of 'Lakefield', Hall Road, Clippesby. Being near the woods and the dykes, everyone was almost eaten alive by the swarms of gnats and midges and the occasional horse fly during the humid summer evenings.

Also of interest, nearly in the centre of the meadow on the east side of 'Lakefield', I remember there stood a huge oak tree, the short trunk of which was enormous, and my brother told me that at one time five men with outstretched arms could not form a completed encirclement. Of course the 'Lakefield' bungalow was not built until many years later by the then land-owner and farmer Wally Kittle.

Clippesby Oak

As Mary has explained, each player had two quoits weighing from two pounds upwards, and to throw a quoit for a distance of twenty yards or more and encircle an iron pin was no mean feat. Strength of arm was needed, but a knack and keen sense of judgement and skill was essential. My friends and I used to play with old horseshoes.

To transport the pair of quoits to a match they would be tied together and slung over the handlebars of a bicycle. We travelled to some away matches as well, cycling of course, and I well remember how we opted for the matches at Martham, where John and I went to the 'Jug and Bottle' and obtained a half of mild beer each – great exceptional joys of those schoolboy days. Some people walked there and back.

I have in my possession two silver medals presented to my father, dated 1930 and 1932, by Aldred and Son, Silversmiths, of Great Yarmouth, and a photograph of the Clippesby team, with Charlie Turner holding the championship cup and Lord Emmley standing in the back row.

Sometimes quite a few supporters assembled at the Clippesby games. Most of them walked, and from the main road and along Hall Road to the farm and outbuildings was a most beautiful vista. The Hall, approached by a winding gravel driveway, was set in a large grassed park, fenced by wrought iron railings to keep the cattle in, and it was lovely to see them roaming about freely and standing in the shade of the large trees which were dotted about. The owner of the Hall at this time was Captain Showell.

At the main road end there stood a triangular-shaped wood on the left side, and a sand pit surrounded by trees on the right, and proceeding along Hall Road, oak and beech trees were planted close together on each side, the tops of which entwined to form an archway above, and even on a hot summer day it was dark and cool. Wrought iron railings were on either side for its whole length, again to keep the cattle in. Rabbits, birds and game were to be seen in great numbers, and wild flowers, primroses, daffodils, violets, etc., were in profusion.

About a quarter way down on the right side, a footpath ran from the road across the field alongside the park, having a stile or kissing gate at each end, and going to Sunday School we always took this path as a short cut to the church. There was a large walnut tree halfway along the path and, needless to say, Captain Showell and his lady did not enjoy many of the nuts, and in retrospect, I sympathise with the church cleaner of that time.

The photograph shows (left to right):
Herbert Hunn, Spencer Whittaker, Lord Emmley, ... (?), William Leggett.
Fred Annison, Gilbert Cooper, Charlie Turner, Stanley Cooper, John Cooper,
Fred Woods.

Marble 'Arter'

Village School, Fleggburgh

If you care to stand at the road gates to Fleggburgh School and cast your gaze to the extreme classroom on the right side of the building, that is where the headmaster reigned supreme and in which pupils in the early 1920s toiled away with their last days of learning before entering out to the big bad world of unknown prospects. A fireplace was situated in the right hand corner by the side of which the head sat at his desk. On the opposite wall which partitioned the adjoining classroom, stood a glass-fronted cupboard which secreted pens, pencils, nibs, paper and various other school necessities and on the middle shelf, taking pride of place for all to see and to remind the unwary to count ten before entering into any foolhardy indiscretions, misdemeanours or whatever, was that instrument of corporal punishment, the three feet of whippy, bendy cane, the thwacks from which I very often and consistently felt throughout the year. It rested tantalisingly like a scorpion resting in a desert boot, waiting for a strike to cause agonising pain.

Outside and alongside the wall of this classroom the ground was of the normal mixed clay and soil, trodden down firmly by countless heavy-soled boots padding to and from the pump room (I'm certain mention of this will bring back memories to a great number of my school friends) which housed an ancient stone-type sink and a 'clacker' pump in which place we took our drinks of water, washed and cleaned the white earthenware inkwells which fitted into the top right hand side of our school desks, mixed the ink powder with water to obtain the right consistency, and, filling the inkwells, carried them back into school to see us through the forthcoming week. This was a pleasant enough chore during the summer months but during the winters of snow and ice, and we always had it year after year, was not in itself a favourable and much-sought-after fifteen to twenty minutes skive from the classroom. However, this was one time when we were allowed to warm our hands by the fire.

However, during the early spring at the start of the marble season, this stretch of path alongside the classroom became the 'holy of holies' and was carefully swept clean of stones and other obstructions by swinging our jackets over and along the entire surface so it was almost like a table top. Whilst the girls skipped, hop-scotched, wearing out their footwear and played ball against the East wall chanting incessant witch doctor wailings, the boys were intent on the school Olympic games of marbles endeavouring to win as many glass 'allys' and marbles as they could. The glass 'allys' which were the main prizes were mostly very beautiful in the varied whirls, loops and blobs of various colours and mixed designs. The dimensional size of these caused them to be 15-20-25-30 or more 'footers' and the lucky owner would sit on the ground with legs wide apart with the prized 'ally' in between and the strikers with their hard baked clay marbles would try and aim correctly to hit and win it. The striking marble was the winner and the 'ally' was claimed and then put up again or substituted for another, in which case the casting distance was altered.

This game was played at every opportunity during the season which only lasted for a few weeks and boys would be seen carrying a special type of poke bag full of marbles. There were lots of tears shed when someone went skint or marble-rupt and fights broke out often. There were probably ten or twelve boys pitching marbles and when one hit the glass 'ally' the others would claim 'marble arter' and a sudden stampede forwards sometimes became catastrophic and included those who were claiming 'marble arter' by false pretences.

126

After school many would sit at home during the evenings, counting, gloating over and admiring their spoils for the day, only to be completely and utterly devastated the following evening when with an empty 'poke bag' the tears would flow easily with the thoughts of what might have been. One could easily understand this because pocket money was not very much and brand new marbles were about eight or ten for an old copper penny and the glass 'allys' anything up to three pence each.

Many were the times in the classroom when a 'marble-rupt' put up his hand, asking, 'Can I leave the room, sir,' not to visit the place for which the permission was granted, but to have a quick 'shufty' alongside the extremities of the marble pitch just in case one or two marbles had escaped the notice of others.

During the hectic season there were bloodied noses, black eyes, cut lips, friendships broken, apples and sweets swopped and the promises, 'I'll give you a ride home on my crossbar for a twenty-footer.'

The most unforgivable sin was to suddenly produce one of the old ground clear-glass bottle stoppers in a swop for the coloured glass 'ally' during the course of the game. Of course this odious person was blacklisted from playing again and was only reinstated into the fraternity after paying his way back in with apples, sweets, promises or worthwhile swops.

As always, adults could be so outstandingly embarrassing during the times when enquiring from a youngster, 'What's up', and the reply, 'I've lorst all me marbles,' and with a hideous and sometimes toothless grin and inane chuckle, 'Never you mind, so hev a lot more'n you,' meaning of course the other definition of the word marbles.

But there is no doubt about the 'friendly' game of marbles whatsoever; we certainly changed the name of the game, and as the saying goes, 'We sartinly took the biscut and a gret ole lump'a that there kearke a'norl'.

One never sees a group of youngsters playing this ancient game these days, I wonder why?

The 1920s Valentine and Pancakes

We have been most fortunate this past month with regard to the weather because in my young and early days I remember the winter months being severely inclement and following Christmas we were usually in the grip of

127

freezing cold winds, snow and sleet, followed by continuous downpours of rain during February and March when the drying of clothes was a great problem for all households.

However, to herald the impending appearance of the Roman goddess 'Flora', the first of our flowers, the snowdrop, struggled through the crusty earth to add a little lustre to our bleak countryside, to be followed by the crocus and in shady, out of the way havens, an early primrose.

Not all was gloom and despondency though; the evening prior to Valentine's Day was quite eventful and hilarious. During the late summer I had gathered lavender, dried it and later sewed it into small gaily-coloured sachets which were adorned with a suitable amorous message and ribbon bow. My other boyish gifts, although laughable now, were of a most delicate and exquisite taste in Valentine sundries, sufficient to arouse the warm affection of any young schoolgirl of the day – to wit, a huge gobstopper which when sucked became a variation of subtle colouring, and two or three aniseed balls purchased at Hudson's shop at ten for an (old) penny.

The semi-detached cottage still stands there, gracing the lower part of Clippesby, just prior to the Loke ,which cuts through to the main top road, (although, not too recently, additional space has been built to either end). Elvina Fuller resided in one and Muriel Gowing in the other (affectionately known as Vina and Muschee respectively), and just as darkness was falling I would venture along the road from my home to deliver my tokens. Not using the gates, which usually squeaked to cause attention, I would nip through a gap in the hedge and thence to the back door, deposit my gift on the doorstep, deafen those inside with loud banging on the door and scuttle quickly behind the shed and await the squeals of laughter and delight emanating from within the respective houses. At school next day there were plenty of sly glances and giggles, and it was surprising what one found inside the school desk.

Also during February I was allowed to make the pancakes for our household on Shrove Tuesday, and this culinary delicacy was much enjoyed by all the family. Bearing in mind the heating of the very heavy iron frying pan was achieved either on the hob of an open fire or on a paraffin stove, I did very well indeed. Starting about the age of nine years, I would mix the batter using two eggs and to the great amusement of my grandfather, would toss them up and over and fortunately only lost the odd one or two. My red post-office money box became a wee bit heavier as it was passed around whilst I was washing up.

George, you all know George, always visits me in the morning and afternoon for tea, and as a treat I asked him to call between half past three and four o'clock last Tuesday and I would cook some pancakes. I wasn't a bit surprised when he walked in at a quarter past three! He was most amused to see me toss them up and over, hoping of course one would end in a crumpled heap on the kitchen floor. The finished product was excellent, with a slight spread of honey, and knowing it is George's nature to crib about something or other – he does not really mean to but it's just his mode of life – I mischievously hid the lemon. He had just started to eat when I enquired if it was all right, and he said, with an 'I've caught you out' look through his spectacles, 'Ha-ha, you've forgotten the lemon!' You should have seen his face when I produced the lemon from its temporary hiding place. He must have enjoyed them though, because he was around again today and we had some more. This is a once-a-year treat and it's back to the fruit cake next week.

Rollesby's Festival of Flowers and Crafts

I am sure that much thought, hard toil and work came to fruition during the last weekend of July when at Rollesby Church FDRC put on their show. Commencing on the Friday evening one was delighted to see the beautiful flower arrangements and during that evening the Lakefield Singers rendered their usual polished performance, and again, as always, how splendid they appeared in black and cream, topped with gold capes. In addition, Cliff Wilson read an amusing story regarding a wayward mole abandoning his spring cleaning. The wind instrumentalists on flute, clarinets and bassoon were also much appreciated. When they came out to play for the second period I whispered to George, 'There's an *oboe* in this

129

time!' and I wondered then why he glanced anxiously over his shoulder to the door and constantly searched the seats with consternation. During a pause in the playing, I suppose unable to constrain himself any longer, he said to me, 'Where is he?' I said, 'Who?' He replied, 'The tramp you saw come in!' I do apologize if my sudden coughing and spluttering in any way upset the audience. It was also a fine gesture, after the events were concluded, that Cliff presented bouquets to Evelyn Chalkley and Mary Cooke, and a gift-wrapped thank-you to the woodwind artists.

On the Sunday afternoon on entering the Church I was confronted with trays of sticky, gooey and sugary cakes and buns and I was compelled to avert my gaze because by just looking I felt I had increased my weight by at least another pound, not that anyone would immediately notice, mind you! Once inside, there were the many and varied exhibits of arts and crafts and professionalism on show. The old manuscripts pertaining to the Church, framed pictures and watercolours were on display, and the original sketches which have appeared in the Parish Magazine were very professionally portrayed by our own Pauline Willmott.

The terrarium plant holders and containers were most impressive and then the tree of life and the oddities prepared by the school children and the Brownies, the outstanding workmanship of the matchstick model maker, with windmill, caravan and clock tower, etc., the sea shells in their various shapes and forms, and the 'Reynard' himself accompanied by an impish grey squirrel, both resplendent in their respective glass cases. There were needlework fancies of all kinds by the over 60s, the lady spinning wool direct from Jacob fleeces, and on display the completed articles of wearing apparel, another lady creating flowers from paper cut-outs and then on to Sally Badham-Thornhill, whose scintillating embroidery in gold and silver threads is magnificent to behold. She was working on the face of a tree trunk and asked if I liked it, and on stating the affirmative I said I could even see an owl in its pop hole, when I promptly had my wrist slapped – it was a knot in the wood! Sorry, Sally, only teasing!!

On display were embroideries of a bittern standing like a sentinel in a reed bed, a water hen, a swallow-tailed butterfly, a frog, and a most magnificent heron, so lifelike were these that it seemed they were indulging in temporary relaxation and one only had to startle them to put them to flight. What a beautiful altar cloth this will be!

Near to the organ another professional displayed her great gifts of artistry – Sandra with her designer clothes in lovely satins and silky textures, and the wonderful creation of the ball gown which, when worn by its owner, did in fact make her the belle of the ball.

We also chatted to a lady who hailed from Swardeston and who as a young girl often spoke to Nurse Cavell. Her husband, organist for 41 years, was engrossed in playing requests. It was such a happy gathering and where there are sounds of music one must eventually sing. Sandra, Cliff and I just couldn't resist the opportunity of a real 'belter' and together we sang, 'How great Thou art', 'Bread of Heaven', 'Crimond', and 'Amazing Grace'. Who could wish for a better conclusion to a splendid afternoon?

Again shielding my eyes from the tantalising eats in the porch and entering the car park, there situate was – an old soldier's life's blood – the 'Char Waggon'; that's organisation for you down to the last letter.

The evening saw us at Deneside, Great Yarmouth, where again the Lakefield Singers were giving a performance, this time sharing the platform with the resident choir. Again the singing was received with pleasure and enjoyed by a medium-sized congregation from as far afield as Scotland and Wembley, Leslie Cooke from Oby and the two young lads from 'the Fine City' and young Sally Pointer from Clippesby of course.

Reaching home at last, it was too early to retire at just gone 11 pm, so I micro rustled a vanilla, walnut and cherry cake for George to enjoy with his cuppa when he visits tomorrow. Normally it would be topped with cream and laced with a layer of jam, but these commodities are devastatingly unkind to the man-about-town figure, so this is now a MUST NOT.

And so to bed...

Rollesby Church

131

The Sunday School Outing.

Just before the end of the summer school holidays, after the harvest had been safely gathered in and whilst the weather was still quite humid and the sun continued to pour its goodness on our rural countryside, then came the Saturday which the children of the village had been talking about for several weeks and hoping and praying it would continue to keep fine for. This was our impending Sunday School treat to Hemsby. As always, the Sunday School numbers had increased just prior to and up to the time when the outing was scheduled to take place, only to drop off drastically after the big day was over and done with.

A wagon and driver with 'Old Dolly' harnessed between the shafts had been provided for the whole day by the local farmer, William Roberts of South House Farm, Clippesby, and was ready and waiting outside Hudson's shop a little after seven o'clock. Old chairs and forms were brought from the home to sit on but mostly everyone sat on the floor which had been liberally littered with fresh straw and still smelling of the new harvest. The area of the floor and space within the wooden sides, which were about three feet in height and surrounded by a ledge all way round supported with iron stays, was always referred to as the 'boke.'

As Old Dolly clip-clopped along, her iron-shoe-clad hoofs resounded off the road surface, how we all wished she would get a bit of a move on and break into a more frenzied clipperty-clop and get us all to the seaside a little bit quicker as the wagon noisily followed her on the iron-tyred wheels which crushed and splintered the small stones and pebbles lying on the road surface.

Passing through the several villages, we waved and shouted to people on the roads, in gardens, and working in the fields and indeed we were a very happy contingent, a wagonload of early life, harbouring great expectations.

On reaching Hemsby after a ride which seemed interminable, we all dismounted and helped carry the baskets and bags of this, that, and the other, to the beach.

Old Dolly would be unharnessed and free to roam and enjoy the lush green grass and vegetation growing on the roadside banks and verges along the narrow road leading to the gap in the sand dunes behind which we could already hear the waves breaking and rustling the shingle on the shore line.

Once on the beach, the deck chairs appeared as if by magic and with all the paraphernalia of those days stacked around them our mothers would settle down for the day. It was then that the Sunday School teacher graciously handed out a shining new half crown to each child with the warning – 'don't lose it or spend it all at once' – but no sooner had it been pressed into an already hot and sticky hand than it was hurriedly in motion and on its way to the ice-cream stall for the first ice-cream of the day.

Our boots and socks off, we roamed along the water line at will, paddling and picking up brightly coloured stones and sea shells and oddments of flotsam and jetsam, all these being placed into a bag for future inspection.

It was when we became peckish and the tummy started to rumble that we turned our thoughts to the ham, cheese, and cucumber sandwiches, and didn't that extra little sprinkling of sand which someone had thoughtlessly sent blowing into the wind, enhance the crunchy effect of the cucumber. But, before we could eat we had somehow to find the source and then came that sudden panicky fear which all children have experienced and encountered at some time or another. We had wandered far along the sea shore and on looking over and along the beach every mother looked the same. There were rows and rows of deck chairs, and all the ladies were wearing long dresses pulled up just as far as the knees and the sleeves of which were rolled only as far as the elbows, but they had taken off their shoes. These were the early days of extreme caution and modesty.

There seemed to be unlimited numbers of those great big floppy brimmed hats, wide enough to cover the shoulders as well. I loved those old hats – I still do – and when I see one being worn these days I always look at the wearer and smile in appreciation for bringing just a glimmer of the olden days into this blatant modern age. In those days these fine hats would cost 'Three eleven three' (3s. 11¾d) and mother sewed on or fastened a few ribbons or flowers; they now cost anything from £30.00 upwards but nevertheless look very adorable and fetching and even on one of our most famous race courses the ardent race-horse owner will turn his gaze to admire another filly in the paddock, wearing a strikingly attractive floppy hat.

However, after eating and drinking our fill, entertainment in the form of a Punch and Judy show would arrive and we would watch this and then away we went again to paddle and dodge the waves as they came rolling in, swishing and stirring the loose shingle at our feet and the ladies would also be paddling with their dresses held up no higher than the knees. Their paddling was termed, 'Doing the feet good.'

It did not seem very long before we were spending the last remaining pennies from our half crown on the coloured sticks of rock to take home and the last one-for-the-road ice-cream.

One last run along the water's edge to rummage for a piece of sea-weed to take home and hang alongside the pine cones as a future weather forecaster and then to the wagon where Dolly was already harnessed within the shafts and waiting in a most happy and relaxed manner.

Not many of us remembered the journey home as we slumbered away on the straw in the wagon, dreaming of our day at the seaside, cucumber sandwiches garnished with a sprinkling of fine sand. Neither did we remember being bathed with a quick lick of the flannel and being put to bed, but such were our hectic and tiring Sunday School treats in the 1920s.

As for Hemsby itself, never did we ever expect it to grow and be as it is now, once a quiet seaside village with some holiday-makers and even the beach changing huts with their giant wheels which were pulled back and forth by horses. No loud music, flashy entertainments, huge holiday camps, flashing lights and continuous noise, noise, noise, but just one of those places of rich beauty, quiet living and a joyous, peaceful serenity.

It would seem that even old Dolly enjoyed her day by the sea, even though she had to pull that lumbering old wagon behind her. What a story she had to tell to Prince, Charlie, and the others that night when she was back at her stable and munching away at a supper of crushed oats and hay for afters. 'Been to the seaside with the kids today chaps, thoroughly enjoyed it. I was presented with Hemsby rock, lumps of sugary cake and apples galore. The grass was plentiful and tasty and I had lots and lots of pats and in return I left several donations of rejuvenator for the roses in someone's garden.'

The Herring Drifters

As a youngster in the early 1920s I would be taken to Great Yarmouth during a shopping expedition and it was customary to always walk along the quayside to marvel at the sight of hundreds of fishing trawlers and herring drifters of the day. The trawlers were much larger and some were powered by steam, whereas the drifters were minute in comparison and were mostly navigated by the use of sail.

These vessels were moored alongside the quay, three and four deep, with the quayside cranes swinging their jibs back and forth from boat to shore, unloading the crans of herring which had been caught. There was continuous shouting and tremendous volume of noise and general hustle and bustle. Horses and carts and vendors pushing barrows and many various types of hand carts seemed to envelop the whole area as they weaved and dodged each other to pursue their individual trades and calling. And this was during the period before the season had properly got under way.

However, we, in company with hundreds of others, were intent on braving the jostling crowds in order to purchase fresh and cheap fish and sometime later we made our way home with 'rush' baskets fully laden with herring at 2d. per dozen.

Down at the South Quay on the spending beach thousands of nets were draped out to dry like washing in continuous stretches of poles where they could be inspected for damage and repairs carried out.

Later, at home, the frying pan on the hob and sizzling away, we enjoyed and relished our participation in a thousand years old industry.

Although herring are caught most of the year in various parts along the coast, the heavy shoals did not arrive off our coast until the autumn and the season was from September until the middle of December or in the common parlance of those days, from the feast of St Michael the archangel until the feast of St Martin. Both the Great Yarmouth and Lowestoft drifters were joined at this time by the Scottish fishermen and the once famous Scottish lassies. They came to prepare the fish for the curing and were dressed in characteristic costume of shawls that formed head scarves, and large aprons. With bare arms they used a specially shaped small knife with a short curved blade and they worked around huge rectangular wooden vats. The unforgettable scene was set against a background of thousands of wooden barrels piled high up and littered with trunks, peds, pots and swills. To watch them gut and clean herring was something which one has never forgotten, the speed, expertise and dextrous manipulation of the knife with which they carried out their monotonous task attracted many onlookers. The herrings, gutted and cleaned, were exported to the Continent and especially to Russia in barrels of brine. It was also ingenious in the way the lassies thrilled the watching onlookers by carrying buckets of water on their heads, unaided by the use of their hands and not even a little 'slop' of overspill.

Not all herrings were dispatched in this way; there was also a booming trade in bloaters when they were caned through the gills and then hung up in their thousands in the smoke houses to be cured. The many old wooden sheds which dotted the shores and outskirts of town added a picturesque identity to the local scene, and the aromas permeating the sea breezes were taken as commonplace.

Truly a great and flourishing industry and right up until the late 50s holiday makers could send home by post boxes of Yarmouth bloaters and kippers, and boxes of 6-12-18 and 24 were dispatched far and wide. To show the great and valuable importance of this humble fish to the Yarmouthians they even incorporated the tails of three herrings in the town coat of arms. Nevertheless, the vast numbers of this species of fish being caught worried me somewhat, and I remember writing an essay at school and putting my thoughts on paper, on which I wrote that the huge numbers caught and then disposed of by other means, other than by feeding the hungry, was not beneficial to the laws of nature. I had noticed for a long time and with trepidation, loads dumped into fields, the countryside smelling awful before they were ploughed in and it was common knowledge that many were the catches which were brought straight from the boats to be rendered into fish meal and manure because there was a surplus and glut. Many were also taken back to the sea and dumped. I poured my heart out on paper and the following day Mr Tweddell, our head master, had a long discussion with me concerning what I had written; I must have impressed him because I won the first prize in English again during that year.

Indeed my schoolboy assumptions were all too correct – where are the herring now? Granted there are still the delicious longshores being caught, but at what a price. The industry folded long ago and the entire length of the quay no longer affords shelter to the small and once prosperous and conspicuous little drifters. They disappeared overnight, or so it seemed, in the same way nature covers its face before the onslaught of an impending storm.

The two small villages of Clippesby and Billockby, two amongst many, shared the traumas of disaster of the once-upon-a-time golden harvest story, and fishermen left their families with a goodbye kiss, never to return. One such fisherman and father was that of a dear friend, George (Jewson) Cooper, his brothers Herbert and Lennie and sisters Gladys and Edith. Samuel Cooper left one afternoon by bus en route for Yarmouth and the little fishing boat he was on never returned.

Most fishermen were Godfearing men, and superstitious to the point of wearing a gold ring in one ear, for had they not seen his wonders of the deep?

Not forgetting the supposedly true utterance from an old sailor assisting in the decorating of his church for the Fisherman's Harvest Festival when one of his friends came in with his hat on, 'Don't you bloody well know where you are?'

The Regatta

After the First World War and regularly every year until I was old enough to know about it, a Regatta was held at Potter Heigham and I remember looking and staring with wonder at the many and varied yachts, sailing

137

boats and other like craft moored alongside each length of the river bank, dressed overall with flags, bunting and other regalia of the day.

For those residing in the immediate vicinity and the scattered villages round about, the Saturday afternoon and evening was the main attraction and purpose for visiting this Mecca in the heart of Broadland, well known far and wide for its small hump-back and cart-track bridge, not only for its simplicity but the folklore surrounding it. You can still see the wooden five-barred farm gate to the entrance of the marsh on the opposite side of the road to the aged corrugated tin amusement centre and fish and chip shop. It was on this marsh that the 1920s showman, a Mr Underwood known to all and sundry as 'Rhubub', pitched his travelling fair. Very modest this was in relation to the fairs and the gadgets of today but we all thought it was wonderful, and so it was. There were the galloping horses, the cake walk, darts, coconut shies, shooting gallery, rolling the penny and hoopla. Always popular were the swing boats in which the young men took a delight in scaring the living daylights from their girl friends by almost standing one of these on its end. Also, too, was the rock and fair-button stall and just as they still are today, the chip and tripe and the shell fish stalls, not forgetting the cornets and the wafers.

When I reminisce about those days, to show the comparison with the present, I remember that with Dorothy Lambert, my schoolgirl next-door neighbour, and my father and mother, we walked from Clippesby to Potter Heigham and after tiring ourselves out at the festivities and full to the brim with ice cream and fair-buttons we then had to walk home through the darkness. It was, and still is, a long trek but no-one thinks about having to walk this distance today. Returning home and to keep off the main road we took to the back lanes from Repps to Ashby and thence to Oby and Clippesby.

Although I was with my parents, there was that great fear and fore-boding which was ever present when darkness fell on and enclosed the rural countryside. Youngsters of my day were continually admonished when being naughty and unruly with, 'If you don't behave I'll tell the bogey man to come and get you,' and in the darkness this fear was multiplied a thousand fold. In later years I looked on Hall Road as a splendid scene of intense and wonderful beauty, when wrought iron railings separated the park from the road, when oaks on either side formed a canopy overhead with their entwined leafy branches, when wild flowers grew in abundance and woods reached right to the verges. When young, however, the

138

overwhelming pitch darkness of cavern-like enormity was most frightening. There were rustles, the whispering of leaves and grasses, the overall noises of a countryside woodland at night. The uncontrollable restlessness of nature and a sudden screech from an owl turned one's blood to a cold trickle.

During the Second World War I felt the same uneasy perception when I was assisting in moving the Guards Armoured Division, whilst on manoeuvres and training to become battle efficient. An armoured convoy stretched for a long distance and Military Police had to be well in front to await the arrival of the first vehicle and after the last one had passed his point on motor cycle, he would then leapfrog to the front of the convoy and take up a position at the next vulnerable road junction. We had made our way from the Yorkshire Moors, were all tired and worn, and on our route back into Somerset, and as I raced ahead and passed the last manned point I came up to a crossroads on Salisbury Plain in Wiltshire where I had to turn the convoy. In the very near distance and barely a stone's throw away stood the always potentially frightening spectre of Stone Henge. I was then well ahead of the convoy and it was dark but with a half moon. Sheep and other cattle were moving about, snuffling and emitting the many noises for which they are renowned and on glancing at that historic monument I felt the same uneasy and uncontrollable fear which I had when walking through the woods and overhanging canopy at Hall Road.

Although I had witnessed many horrific scenes whilst in combat action, this was something entirely different; it was the past, lifting itself from the soil with the Druids raising their skinny arms to the moon in prayer, and although I tried to console myself that this was the past legacy of the inherent 'bogey man' never had I been so pleased to hear the distant rumble of tank tracks and then to see the swirling clouds of dust caused by them obliterating that awesome scene.

You may think to yourselves, fancy him making all that fuss about Stone Henge. But then again I suppose that those of you who have seen it visited during the daytime and then in company with others. I challenge you, wait till there is a half moon, then go and visit it, entirely on your own. If there is a slight trace of mist and the shadows are wavering with the movement of the clouds overhead causing silhouettes and images to dance in and out of the gigantic pillars in the stillness and quiet, you will then hear the beating of your own heart. It is then you will feel that coldness in bodily temperature when your mind tells you, you are witnessing imaginary images of skinny people proffering themselves.

Getting back to the Regatta, not until I got my first bike did I witness the actual sailing, and then the only interest in it was to watch the races until a boat turned turtle and to then watch the resultant commotion. Unfortunately, there is no Regatta today and as far as I can trace, way back in 1964 the 65th annual turnout had reached the end of its useful time. Support had fallen off, particularly from the sailing fraternity. Also, support from other individual Regattas which, apart from Potter Heigham, had faded out completely. One reason was the lack of people with private sailing craft going round the various venues towing one or two sailing boats.

On 17th February 1964 a Committee meeting voted 21 out of 35 present for another try, and a crisis meeting was held at the Broadshaven Hotel on March 9th of the same year.

Then occurred another void in the Broads sporting calendar.

The Fair Engines

During the 1920s regattas, fêtes, fairs and markets were held around our parishes of the Fleggs, and Great Yarmouth was then our principal town for entertainment and shopping. Palmers and Arnolds were household names.

The Saturday jaunt to Great Yarmouth Market, where locally grown produce was on display, was frequent for those who did not own large gardens or have access to an allotment and there were three or four market gardeners from the Fleggburgh area who displayed fruit and vegetables on their stalls which was said to be 'Sitting Market.'

The highlight of attending the 'Pictures' was when long queues formed alongside the chip stalls to purchase, then salt and vinegar, the luscious chips, and it was common knowledge that these were of the best in the country and many still say the same thing today. I never did go much on the accompanying 'tripes, chitlins and scratchins,' well, they come from the inside, don't they?

Once every year the Market Place was taken over by the Fair which provided one of the main attractions for all peoples from around a wide area of the neighbourhood, and naturally enough all the youngsters loved it for beside enjoying the many activities we could fill up with the aforementioned chips etc., in addition to the fair-buttons, rock and ginger beer from the pop stall.

Prior to this, the Fair had been sited at Norwich on the extensive Cattle Market, opposite the Shirehall, for the period of Easter Saturday and Monday. Then, on the Wednesday, we knew that most of the larger attractions, all packed up and placed on huge trailers and drawn by one of the beautiful steam locomotives, would be passing by Billockby Corner en route to Great Yarmouth and we would wait for and watch these magnificent engines pass by, towing three and sometimes four trailers. These engines were imposing in appearance, power and ability and their total build-up was much greater in proportion than that of their cousins, the tractor engines, which plied themselves to the threshing machines and other varied agricultural needs. They were painted and lined with red, gold and other bright colours and the roof, which covered the main bodywork and stoke-hole in which the driver stood, was also gaily painted, the lapped sides of which portrayed the owner's name, that also in nicely painted letters, and the whole supported by twisted brass stanchions highly polished. The big rear wheels, about six feet in height, were shod with solid and durable rubber tyres and again the hub and spokes were gaily painted.

On the front structure sat a cylindrical shaped generator dynamo which provided sufficient electrical power to operate the lights and energy for which ever attraction the owner had chosen. Somewhere about the engine, but easily seen and read, was the name given to the handsome giant and mostly this was feminine. As it passed by us there was no aggressive noise, which one would have expected, but just a gentle puffing from the smoke stack and a quiet hissing of escaping steam.

Moments later it was gone, soon to be out of sight after rounding Billockby Hall bend.

One or two boys would then lay down with ears pressed to the road surface and report that another engine was proceeding over Acle Bridge or along the causeway and we would then wait for the next engine to approach and pass by.

Whether this method did truly work or not was debatable, but one thing was very much evident and that was 'one lug 'ole' being very filthy indeed with its constant contact with the road surface.

Sometimes we would gather at the Stokesby Road turning where an engine would be stopped to take on water. Out came the long hose with its weed-catching basket attached and then lowered into the wide dyke. There were many loud noises of gurgling, rumbling and disgruntled sounds inside the copper tummy and the emission of an occasional belch as the tank was being filled, and once completed the hose was wound up and hung on the hook attached to the outside of the coal bunker. A couple of whistles then rent the air, as much as if to say, 'I enjoyed that,' and then noiselessly it slipped away on its ten mile journey.

On the Saturday afternoon and evening we would be at Great Yarmouth and again watch and marvel at the prowess of the engines which we had seen earlier, now showing off their full working power, the continuous humming of the dynamo generator pouring out all the electricity needed for the several amusements.

Later on, biking home, broke and full up to the chin with cockles, chips, fair-buttons, ice cream and pop, none of us had lights on our bikes but we were wily country creatures and knew where the policemen would be in their relation to meeting points and when, on hailing a passer by, 'Hi mister, seen any coppers about?' the answer was in the negative, we carried on, but remember, in those days there was very little traffic and when a vehicle came up from behind we dismounted.

Somewhere along the route home we would pass the point where the local police would be meeting for conference; we knew the respective locations and dismounted well before and announced our approach with excited laughter and talk but once past we knew it was then safe to get on and ride and the fear of being taken to Rollesby Court House and fined 5/- for riding a cycle during the hours of darkness without displaying a white light to the front and a red light to the rear was dispelled. In later life, the escapades and small misdemeanours committed by myself and friends made me tolerant to the misdeeds of others and very often I found that a little talk and a caution would suffice for the occasion.

Such excursions as this played a great part in the leisure of our young lives, it was great fun, non-expensive and simple but very rewarding and we were satisfied with that which we had, but in any case we had to be, there was no earthly use for a constant cry of 'I want this, I want that,' because we did not get it!

'Fare ye well tagather – nites be pullen in agin, ent tha.'

The *Albion*

Last week I visited a large store in Norwich City and in the packing shop I saw two items on the floor which immediately brought back a vivid vista of nostalgia. In my own mind I was certain that what I was looking at were two pulley blocks and tackle, complete with the hand-forged snaffle hooks. Close by was a part of an old winch which I guessed had at some time or other, in the faded past, accomplished the strength and muscle power to raise the heavy black sail of a wherry. I was always of the opinion that the most striking feature of a wherry was, of course, her huge black sail which had been dressed with a thick coating of fish oil and tar. The experts will tell you there has never ever been another rig with the unique quality of being able to sail into the eye of the wind, having no like or equal in navigating the numerous river bends. There was one single halyard with the ropes attached to the winch, the forward edge of the sail roped to staunch wooden rings that circled the massive mast.

It is thought that the wherry developed from a much smaller craft of about five tons and most probably during the 17th century and by the middle of the 19th century it was estimated over three hundred trading wherries on our Norfolk rivers traded for hire.

Wherries were of course exclusively built to be trading vessels and carriers of goods in the early days of passengers and sail from Great Yarmouth and also between the out-of-the-way Broadland villages. Even the City of Norwich owed much of its early prosperity to the wherries, which seemed to provide the only safe, fast and regular transport to the coast for the ever-growing wool trade.

The largest wherry ever built is said to have been the *Wonder,* carrying a burden of 90 tons. Mostly they were clinker built with a tall mast of pitch pine or larch of some 40 ft. in height and as it had to be raised or lowered by one man with a minimum of effort and the maximum speed, it was stopped well forward and pivoted in a tabernacle of tremendous strength and then counter-balanced with a weight of two tons or more.

The deck of the wherry was entirely free from all encumbrances so that the wherryman could, if the wind failed or became foul, quant the vessel along. The quant was a long pole with a spike and shoe on one end to hold a grip on the river bed and a shaped shoulder piece at the other and the wherryman, whilst pushing hard, walked the length of the deck from stern to stern, thereby being a means of progress. It could be, and indeed was, very hard work when navigating against both wind and tide. The major capacity of the hull was taken up by one long hold for the cargo but in the stern was a small cabin for the crew and a well from which the vessel was worked. They had a draught of less than four feet of water, allowing penetration into places where other vessels could not enter, again emphasising their extraordinary uses, but in spite of this, had a fantastic carrying capacity and it was quite a normal function to sail with the midship decks awash. The large wherries traded along the waterways of the Broads for 250 years and were the undisputed workhorses for all goods and chattels on these waters, but they were doomed to become obsolete.

The railways came and took the cream of the trade; steam and petrol took over from sail and by the end of the 19th century the wherries had lost the battle. Their timbers can still be seen in some of the backwaters throughout Broadland, one of the more mute tributes to the progress of man. It is also natural that the railways, which first started the decline, are, and have been, facing the same challenge from road transport.

The 1914-18 war brought a short respite to those few trading wherries which were left, but World War II saw them off for good – but not all of them; the joy and majesty of my boyhood days, the *Albion* was to be reprieved. She was built in 1898 and was the last trading wherry on the Broads but even this old lady was feeling the impetus of 'rhumatiks, lumbergo and arthuritus' and then the gods of waterways, in the guise of the Norfolk Wherry Trust, preserved her and she was restored in 1949. She is still navigable and has cost a lot of money, and if she is still to exist, will cost a lot more. As a trading vessel she has seen the end of the line and it is a struggle for the Trust to raise the necessary for repairs and maintenance.

As she is the end of the line, the Broads will lose a crucial link with their history of the last 300-350 years. If she has to give up, it would be suitable for her to be given a place of honour, somewhere on Broadland, with the same priority as that given to the *Victory* at Portsmouth. Incidentally, when Nelson was learning to sail on the Barton Broad, there were then in excess of 300 wherries afloat and, not having brakes, I wonder how many of these large vessels he bumped into?

If you were to see the *Albion* today, she would not be the same vessel which I knew in my schooldays, when I would wait at the moorings near Acle bridge. When the large sail had to be lowered I would hail the skipper, and he would steer close to the pilings and I would jump on and have a trip round the Acle bend towards Thurne. Sometimes I would be dropped off at a convenient landing spot so that I could make my way home across the marshes, but sometimes, with a bit of boyish persuasion, would stop off at the top of Thurne dyke and I would then walk along the river wall to the village and home – a very long walk indeed – but what memories it conjures up.

In those days there were all the intermingled pungent smells from the fish oil and tar on the sail, the smoke fumes from the little cabin stove, the sweat from the men and the many more smells from the various cargoes.

Today she has been modified, the inside so spick and span with aluminium and steel-topped tables and shelves, and is used for trips of pleasure. This is not the old 'grandmama' I once knew, but then progress marches on and most unfortunately this beauty and serenity seldom go like young lovers, hand in hand.

There is always some little nicety to be found and which comes to hand in every sphere of life, and one in relation to the wherries, is that, and I quote 'In spite of their shallow draught they had a fantastic carrying capacity and it was quite normal to sail with the midships awash.' Actually, I have heard it said, that a wherry was not properly loaded unless a robin could drink off the deck.

I just wonder who the person was who could envisage such a fatuous assumption.

A 1920s Christmas

We have broken up from school and everyone is agog with the expectations of Christmas. A blur of thin snow has fallen, and across the fields to the marshes the hedgerows show up in sharp relief against the stark white landscape, and the dykes, not yet completely frozen over, form images and appear like miniature roadways on the freckled face of a map. Snow is beautiful in its own way and as I gaze over the fields I can see it swept into the shapes of small furrows and irregular mounds by the freezing cold winds blowing in from the North.

The front room is ready; in these days it is only put to use on high days and holidays and anyone coming along to Sunday tea, and this Christmas was one of those occasions. The tree was already in the corner, and, amazingly, notwithstanding a terrible fire risk, miniature candles in crocodile type clip-holders were placed and lit amongst the paper trimmings and baubles. Everyone was on good behaviour and contrary to the other days of the year, except on approaching birthdays and outings, it was, 'Yes, Mum – no, Mum,' – what little creeps we were and the gobstoppers just wouldn't melt in our mouths!

After tea on Christmas Eve there was none of the usual hanky-panky about going to bed; the apprehension and excitement was so acute, with the adrenalin flowing, it happened with one formal request. And so, up the wooden hill to bed, with Mother leading the way with a lighted candle; we had to have a light as we saw a tramp on the top road today, and you never

146

know! On hands and knees, I had a thorough good searching look under the bed – I didn't want anyone under there to frighten Father Christmas or pinch my presents! Then I had one look at the fireplace, moving the fireguard to one side just in case he should be in a bit of a hurry and knock it over, waking me up. But then, again, I was thinking, he's going to get awfully dirty – I had overheard Mother saying to Dad, 'We'll have to get Teddy Debbage in to sweep the chimney after Christmas.' One last thing to do – I secured a large pillow case to the bedpost nearest the fireplace, and leapt into bed. 'Goodnight Mum,'– and then the all-embracing darkness surrounded me as the candle left the room. For several minutes I lay around tormenting myself – would he forget where I lived – had someone told him I had thrown stones and knocked off all the insulating cups from the telephone posts down the road – did he know I had cheeked poor old 'Nobby' Clark as he came home from work in his donkey cart and had tried to entice the donkey to pull up whilst holding out a carrot? Did...? had...? would...?

I was awake early, before it was light, in fact, and not being allowed matches or candle I had to content myself with feel and rattle, and soon located a tin of toffees and a huge orange. 'Coo,' I thought to myself, 'he's been!' When the light dawned I noticed lots of things – the fireguard was back in its rightful place – I wonder how he did that? – and not a bit of soot about anywhere, he must have brought his own dustpan and brush – and my white pillowcase with toys and things – not a bit of soot on it anywhere. Ha-ha, I noticed also the glass of whisky Grandfather had left on the mantelpiece had gone.

Funny thing about the whisky, though, because the other night I had had a perplexing dream, that I was all 'growed' up and approaching the age of borrowed time, and standing out near our road gate I saw an unsteady Santa being escorted away by two men in strange uniforms. The sled was overturned and broken, and the reindeer were in Mr Jack Key's field, nibbling away at his winter barley. The men intimated the sled would be confiscated and the reindeer impounded for at least twelve months. Funny dreams we have – whatever did they mean by 'endorsement' and 'disqualification'? I overheard them talking about excess alcohol in Santa's breath, and that an intoximeter test showed he had 105 microgrammes of alcohol in 100 millilitres of breath. What did all this mean?

They wore white caps with a black and white chequered band; and you should have seen the beautiful cream-coloured large mobile unit they had!

It was completely surrounded with a red and blue band, which, when caught in the light showed up in fluorescent colours, whilst a rotating blue light was flashing away on its rooftop, creating an awesome spectacle. What's more, although there was no-one in this fantastic vehicle, I heard a series of pips and definitely someone calling out for 'Delta 32' and then 'Charlie 7'. And then I saw huge red and white ice-cream cones growing out of the road! I mustn't read that book by H. G. Wells any more before going to bed. I shall not be mentioning this to anyone, because I'm only ten years old and I don't want to be sent away to one of those places!

Nevertheless, what a lovely day we all had; my big sister Hilda was home for the holiday, and we enjoyed a lovely traditional dinner and tea, after which we sat around the table playing whist and Newmarket. I liked Newmarket because I could cheat a little bit! I always came off best, win or lose, being the youngest member of the family, and my money box once again had that pleasing rattle coming from within.

What a beautiful illusion this time of year brings for a child – but it is not until a little bit later that he or she comes to grips with the true reason for this annual celebration. But for now it wouldn't be long before we would once again be trudging along that weary, uneven road to school; the snow would still be evident, an icy wind sweeping across the marshes and fields and icicles hanging from the hedgerows like crystal decorations, the starkly leafless, naked trees taking on a most forlorn and lifeless portrait. The miracle of spring was yet to come, but what mattered was, we were in another year and, following our Christmas-tide, I was now a year older.

Thoughts after the storm

The recent high winds which caused so much devastation and havoc during the night of Thursday, 15th October, 1987, left its mark on our English countryside, towns and cities, and also yawning gaps in our pleasant landscape. Our younger people of today, in future years, will be relating and writing about this night in our history and telling of the terrible destruction caused to buildings, trees and a myriad of objects we looked upon as commonplace, but which cannot ever be replaced. No gas or electricity, 147 of our national roads blocked and cut off to commuters and vehicles, minor roads impassable, our homes, fields and land flooded, train and bus services unable to operate, our ships in safe anchorage and aeroplanes grounded.

It reminds one with stark realisation that man can devise and achieve many and marvellous things to enhance and improve our civilisation, also to destroy it, but in all his wisdom and present-day education, is unable to combat and can do very little to harness the elements and the seas. He cannot emulate, only provoke, Genesis. It also makes one reflect on the conceit of men who think they rule the world with computers and technological skills, and it only takes something like this to prove what nature can achieve when she gets angry, leaving vast reserves untouched.

Following this night we all saw sights which saddened us, and prompted many to ask, 'How? Why?' From the many poignant scenes I witnessed there is one which I think about the most and which affects me in memory only. Every time I visited Clippesby and made my way along the road from Billockby Corner towards South House Farm, there in the distance was the magnificent red-topped barn standing out for all to see, and dwarfing the cluster of smaller farm buildings in its immediate vicinity. But, alas – no more!

I myself knew it to be in its third generation of ownership; firstly William Roberts, followed by Jack Key, and presently Mrs M. Alston, and this only covers the period from the 1920s. I remember when it sported a fine and impressive thatched roof, and as a boy I would climb the walls of the adjacent bullock yards, shin up the gable end wall, and on reaching the ridge would sit astride it and move along from end to end. It was a very high barn, and having attained my lofty position, I would be treated to an excellent view and panorama all round, especially over the marshes to the river. On clear, fine days I could see the causeway and Acle Bridge. I would sit there for long periods watching the cattle on the marshes, the windmills and movements on the River Bure.

In the days when, after harvest had been gathered in and the stackyards were full and resplendent with ten or more huge corn stacks, the threshing tackle with its steam engine, drum and straw pitcher would be hired, during and after the winter months, and the corn would be placed in the barn, either in sacks or loose on the floor, reaching high up the walls, I remember seeing tons of wheat, barley and oats in this barn.

Also during the winter months it would house loads of swedes, turnips and hay to feed the bullocks which were brought into the yards for fattening.

What a great pity this splendid old building is no more, and will no longer grace the skyline; but for myself, it will always be there, and with its thatched roof. No doubt if I stop and ponder long enough, I will still be able to conjure up and envisage a small mischievous boy, sitting high up astride the ridge.

High Barn, Clippesby, partially demolished in the gale of October 1987

WARTIME MEMORIES

The Geography Lesson

About 1926-27, I sat in Mrs Bracey's class at Fleggburgh School (every-one will undoubtedly remember Mrs Bracey) and during the geography lesson we were studying the Middle East which would eventually be included in the class examinations. I was then seven or eight years of age and I remember how, on reading about and seeing the pictures of the great pyramids and sphinx at Giza, I wished I could one day not only go there and see them to gaze and ponder on their massive enormity, but to touch the huge cut and hewn rocks which had stood there for about 6,000 years. Then again, were they not one of the Seven Wonders of the World? At this time in my life it was only to be an impossible dream; in no way would the circumstances of the day in question permit the resources available to explore this adventure, and I comforted myself with the reading material of that which the Pharaohs had accomplished and became totally engrossed with the photographs appearing in my geography book.

Even after I left school and went into the Army, the lingering and tormenting thoughts were still with me and I then had hopes that by some chance I might be posted to Egypt, but later learned that this was not one of the exotic countries in which my Regiment would be fortunate enough to serve, India yes, but not my Egypt. However, I did go to Gibraltar during the time of the Spanish Civil War, where at intervals from our vantage point on the Rock we could follow certain aspects of their national struggle from across the Bay of Algeciras and at the North Front Barrier to La-Linea, but at Gib. I was a long, long way off Egypt but was able to visit Tangier from time to time.

Then came the traumatic years of the Second World War and much to my personal bodily cost I saw active service in France and Belgium and it was nearly 1½ years before I recovered sufficiently to resume an active part in the service which I had chosen.

Shortly after this with a draft of 63 others, I was moved to a large hotel in London which had been taken over as accommodation for about 1,000 men. We were vaccinated, inoculated, pricked and prodded and early one morning without prior warning were ordered to be ready in 15 minutes to board a troop train. Taking stock of our surroundings I realized we were making towards the south coast. No one had been told even a whisper as troop movements were very hush-hush; no prior home leave had been granted and nor were there any facilities to write or post a letter. We eventually arrived at Southampton Docks, were hurriedly ordered aboard a troopship and within a short space of time were moving out through the Solent, into the English Channel and thence to the unfriendly and wild Atlantic Ocean. There we met up with and joined a convoy of merchant ships of all shapes and sizes and for obvious reasons our troopship was given a favourable position in the centre of the convoy. We were all aware and knew of the menace of the lurking underwater 'U' Boats and it was comforting to see the escorts of Royal Naval Destroyers speeding around the extremities of the convoy but apprehension and strain showed on the faces of all. After the second day at sea the tannoy system rattled out the purpose of our sudden departure from London; we were destined as reinforcements for the 1st and 8th Armies.

Zig-zagging to try and foil the 'U' Boats, there were several terrible periods when some of our convoy were hit and sunk by torpedoes and it was a most nerve-destroying and traumatic sea journey. However, after making our dangerous passage through the rough waters of the bay of Biscay, past the coasts of Portugal and Spain, through the straits of Gibraltar, where in the not so far distance I could see the Buena Vista Barracks, behind Europa Point, where I had been happily stationed during 1937-38, and thence into the beautiful Mediterranean. We saw the Island of Malta in the far distance and mostly, excepting for the daily practice of boat drill, were able to watch and enjoy the antics and play of the friendly porpoises keeping up with and happy in the presence of our company. We eventually arrived and disembarked at the Port of Alexandria in Egypt and I thought to myself then – so near yet so far from the pyramids because the 8th Army was then fighting its way over the desert in the opposite direction.

How often have you heard it said that fate takes a mean advantage over one's existence and life's destination, and true to this saying my draft of 63 found ourselves at the R.M.P. Transit Camp in a place named Abbassia – just about 15 miles from Cairo. We were graciously given time to develop and recover from the excruciating pains and discomfort and emission from both ends with the violent eruptions of the well known 'Gyppo Tummy' with which everyone unfortunately had to come to grips.

On receiving our orders, at first I could not believe or comprehend my enormous stroke of luck with the news that 27 were posted to the 1st Army, 27 to the 8th Army and the odd 9 to bolster up the resources in Cairo, and I was on my way to Cairo.

We worked in pairs in Cairo and my other half and I on the first available day rode on the fast Metro tram to the Giza Plateau where sat the two great pyramids of (K) Cheops and Chephren and a short distance away from which rested and crouched the legendary Sphinx. The massive structures could be seen just after leaving Cairo and never before had I ever experienced such a feeling of joy and a tummy full and teeming with excited butterflies. On arriving there I touched and leaned against the object of my schoolboy fascination and as if in complete topsy-turvy, Clippesby and Fleggburgh School were now far away in the world of distance as I was now here with one of the Seven Wonders of the World – built of more than 2.3 million limestone blocks weighing 2½-15 tons each, 480 feet high, 740 feet square with the base lengths only 6/10s of an inch out of true and the square angle with a 12 sec. error only, and, remember, all this without the aid of precision instruments.

I visited the site many times during my stay in Cairo and clambered up the side of Cheops almost every time I went there and even into the centre of the pyramid, which was quite claustrophobic, but an experience which was not to be missed. There is only one word to describe the view from the top of the great pyramid – fantastic, and Pharaoh-provided. The top twenty feet of Cheops had been lowered and a scaffolding pole of the same height affixed with wires to the four sides, and being young, I suppose, and foolhardy, I pulled myself to the top and scored my initials on the very top of the pole just to prove I had been to the very top of the pyramid, without even a thought of the National News which would have exploded had one of the supporting wires snapped under my weight. I understand that the climbing has long since been banned owing to the wear and erosion of the blocks. Although I visited many world-renowned features – the Citadel lined inside entirely with beaten gold, the Egyptian State Museum wherein lie the fabulous and priceless treasures of the boy king, Tutankhamen, walking and stopping at the stations along the Way of the Delarosa and making the Pilgrimage to Bethlehem and Jerusalem, wading through the River Jordan, and many more – my schoolboy longing had been accomplished. Most of my friends hated the Middle East with its squalor and dirt, disease and flies but to me it held a fascination and I loved it, staying out there for 5½ years, able even to hold a conversation in the Arabic tongue, and now I often reproach myself for not pursuing it further. Whilst there, censorship on letters continued and I could not let my family know where I was until I remembered my mother knew my favourite poem was that of 'Vitae Lampada', the torch of life, and in one letter I wrote, 'For the sake of conscience read the second verse of my favourite poem', and of course she knew exactly where I was because it begins, 'The sand of the desert.' Lately, I have that same irrepressible schoolboy urge once again to see the pyramids and before very much longer I shall be off again, only this time, under totally different terms and will not stay for quite so long a period, also not to obtain my near-to-black suntan.

The Keys of St Peter

Early in the 1920s, when I was chin high to a dandelion, I can recall being pushed up and down the road in my kiddie cart to attend the Easter and Harvest festivals in the days when the entire village filled the church to capacity. Our route would take us as far as Hall Road and along it to where the iron railings separated Clippesby Hall Park from the adjoining field, alongside which ran a footpath leading directly to the church porch.

155

These were mostly sunny days and I remember even at that tender age how my attention was constantly drawn to the coloured spectacle of the keys of St Peter, one silver crossing one of gold, moulded into the right-hand top quarter of the east window above the altar and reredos. They held an unusual fascination for me, and even in later years when attending Sunday School I was often admonished for not paying attention when my eyes were seen to be diverted to the top right-hand quarter of that east window. I could not have explained this irresistible influence captivating my mind even if I had been asked to do so.

Some few years later, having no prospects of employment in the rural area of the Fleggs, and not wishing to be an extra drag on the resources of my family, at the ripe old age of just over 15 years, I joined the elite ranks of the Norfolk Regiment with the 2nd Battalion, in the Band and Drums. Because I was tall and well-built I was trained as the Bass (Big) drummer and enjoyed the privilege of such great momentous occasions as the Aldershot Tattoo, Olympia, and other massed band events. I still remember the 20th January, 1936, when King George V died, and the 22nd January when we led the battalion in London whilst they lined the streets for the proclamation of King Edward VIII, and again on the 28th January for the funeral procession of King George V.

In 1937 we moved to Gibraltar where life in the sun was most enjoyable, although at the time the Spanish Civil War was being fought, but in September 1938 when the shadow of war fell over Europe during the Munich crisis, we were responsible for guarding the barrier gate into Spain, via La Linea, and for the first time since 1918 steel helmets were worn and ammunition issued whilst on guard in real earnest.

We returned home in 1938 after stopping off at Malta for a short break, and found we were again in the Aldershot Command, stationed at Bordon, when with great trepidation and a little apprehension on the 3rd September 1939 we learnt we were once again at war with Germany.

The Battalion arrived at Cherbourg on 21st September 1939 when it suddenly struck me very forcibly that the 2nd Inf. Div, of which we were then part, had the distinctive logo of 'two crossed keys', and instinctively I thought of our own little church and realised this appeared to be a good omen. With such a coincidence facing me I said to myself, 'Jimmy boy, this surely means you will come through this all right.'

During the phoney war we were billeted in the small town of Orchies, when on the 9th-10th May there was considerable enemy air activity and

156

bombs fell on and around us, and the battalion was ordered to move across the Belgian frontier and take up a new defensive line. By that evening we had concentrated at Beuvry Nord in the Forêt de Marchienne, when our C.C. informed us we were to form part of the advance to the Division and were to occupy the wooded slopes behind the river near Wavre, a small town about twenty miles from Brussels. I shall never forget his words, 'We have now reached a stage where we will go forward to meet our enemy; now more than ever before should your previous training stand you in good stead. I wish you all good luck, and remember from now on when you aim to shoot, you aim to kill.' Shortly after, in the darkness, we moved forward, but not without trepidation, as we thought on those ominous words of portent. But, this was war.

I will spare you the trauma of a soldier in action, of dreadful scenes of carnage, death and destruction, the now and again 'roll calls', during lapses in fighting, when on glancing around one could define the decimated numbers and be thankful to answer 'Here' when your number and name was called, wondering would there be a next time? But somehow I always consoled myself I had that extra canopy of faith surrounding me.

Such a lot occurred which is forever burned into the memory, and I remember on the evening of 16th May we were ordered to retire to Lothe on the Brussels-to-Charleroi Canal. The roads through the forest of Soignes were confusing and in the darkness we marched for 17 miles and when I sometimes hear people say it is impossible to march in one's sleep I have to laugh because I am the living proof that this can and did happen.

Being subjected to bombing, shelling, machine-gun fire and close fighting, and getting only small snatches of sleep, on 20th May we made a stand which was to be my last useful contribution to the 2nd (Crossed Keys) Div. of the B.E.F. We had moved to a defensive position along the River Escaut at Tournai and one could see the Germans forming up for attack and, as records point out, 'After first light on the 21st, 'A' Company (my company), being the first to be attacked. It began with heavy mortaring which caused numerous casualties. The heavy fighting continued on and during the 22nd and, undeterred by extremely heavy casualties caused by machine-gun and rifle fire to the enemy, twice more they broke the battalion line, and twice more they were driven back.'

During the afternoon of 22nd May there were just four of us left in my platoon and we had taken temporary cover in a disused cement factory when I crossed the floor to check our left flank, and – 'Whoomf'! – I hit the

157

ceiling and fell to the floor seriously wounded in the left leg and thigh. I was plugged and tourniqueted and placed in the lee of a railway track, where a hundred yards to my right were my H.Q. and stretcher-bearers. Unable to walk, I was forced to crawl alongside the track, but the rails afforded me the cover from machine-gun and rifle fire which passed over me. With my battledress ripped to tatters I carried on for what seemed a lifetime; being near to exploding aircraft bombs I was several times covered and partly buried with dirt and rubble. By crawling over the rough ground my hands and fingers were torn and bleeding and when again I was covered by a bomb blast, being so weak and then uncaring I said, 'Please help me!' I don't know how much later, I vaguely recall being pulled by my arms and then later looking up to see an M.O. and a nun bending over me, and then the welcome degree of oblivion which the drug morphine brings.

On reaching the beaches of Dunkirk I was stretchered aboard the hospital ship *St Julian* and although painted in brilliant white with huge red crosses on decks and hull, she was being bombed and machine-gunned relentlessly – so much for the Geneva Convention – but more morphine would have eased any distress or panic if we had been sunk.

I arrived at the Royal Sussex County Hospital, Brighton, on 29th May, where teams of surgeons performed their many marvellous feats of medical skill on all of us, and later on I pondered over my deliverance, and even today I am fully convinced that someone had been watching over me. I was still only 20 years of age.

I progressed slowly and on Saturday, 29th June, 1940, I was in a wheelchair when I was told by my operating surgeon that I had indeed been a very fortunate and *lucky* boy coming through a million to one chance, and that I would walk again.

I subconsciously noted this date to dwell on during the future, and shortly after was overcome by its significance when looking through a reference diary. I just could not believe my eyes – do you know what this date is, without looking it up? – let me tell you: it is ST PETER'S DAY.

I have often spoken about this eventful episode which embraced the darkest period of my life, and have been met with cynicism; have been told it was just pure luck, etc., etc. Some say the coincidence is much too deep to have doubts, but for myself I still believe there is something more.

By the way, the hospital ship *St Julian* returned to Dunkirk and being fully loaded was sunk by enemy bombing on its return to England.

I know that some time in the future the day must come when I will be in front of the crossed silver and gold keys in our east window for the last time, and I do hope the sun is shining through and portraying that outstanding image which to me, has meant so much since childhood.

My Comrades

Late in 1939 I crossed over to France in a large and ungainly paddle steamer, the *Royal Daffodil* with other men of my battalion. It did not take us long to make the crossing and we landed at Boulogne within a short time. On Saturday, 28th (?) 1990, with veterans of the Norfolk and Norwich 1940 Dunkirk Veterans Association, I crossed the Channel once again in an up-to-date and supposedly fast ferry service. We were at Dover well on time and should have sailed at 2.15 pm to Calais. Later we were diverted to Folkestone from which place we left at 9.30 pm for Boulogne, eventually arriving at our hotels in Ostend at 3.30 am, a good start to our 50th anniversary of deliverance from the beaches of Dunkirk.

We who were fortunate enough to be present on this history-making pilgrimage recalled the many incidents and events which are forever in the recesses of our compassionate thinking and above all remember the great

159

spirit of the time and the many comrades who are sadly no longer with us. The ceremonies which formed part of the pilgrimage gave us all an opportunity to reflect on a major incident of history and additionally upon our own lives and God-given good fortune.

Following the ever-lengthening speeches and parade at Dunkirk, everyone proceeded to the beaches, but we had anticipated the crowds of holiday-makers and sight-seers and so went to the small French town of Uxem where we were welcomed by the Lady Mayoress and townspeople. We were fêted and the champagne flowed. Just outside the town a new road had been named after one of their renowned citizens and they had held back the ceremony for weeks so that we could join them in celebration.

Later during the afternoon we made our way back to the Dunkirk Cemetery but the holiday crowds had still not dispersed and it saddened us to watch them running over and trampling on graves, throwing down their rubbish as if this was a seaside venue. Didn't someone once say, 'Forgive them for they know not what they do.'

On the morrow we were up bright and early and made our way to Le Paradis, the small village where 97 of our battalion were ruthlessly massacred by the German S.S. On arrival at the barn, at which place they first of all surrendered, we found a large crowd awaiting us and were astounded to find a brand new memorial erected by the French people in their honour. They have also nominated the barn to be a place to be preserved for posterity. At this site I was called upon to sound the Last Post and Reveille, and after the short service a very elderly gentleman approached me and said, 'You did very well under extreme stress, but take heart, I taped the ceremony and your bugle calls and a copy tape will be sent to the British Imperial War Museum to be placed in the archives.'

Following this a wreath-laying service was held at the farm where the massacre took place and again I was privileged to sound the Last Post and Reveille. Then on to the Church for another service where a beautiful ancient and heavy brass candlestick about three and a half feet tall was handed over to the pastor. This was a truly beautiful object which was given to our branch by a benefactor and which would have graced the interior of any great Cathedral or Church but we decided to present it to this small place of worship and to the people who pray there and who have done so much for us. Again, inside the church, I was called upon to render the Last Post and Reveille.

After this emotional service was concluded, we paraded outside the Church where stands our own branch-erected memorial on ground given to us by the village. A huge crowd had gathered and again wreaths were laid, after which three French trumpeters and I sounded the Last Post and Reveille alternately. By this time my lips were beginning to feel a trifle rubbery and although somewhat anxious I did manage to complete the two calls without faltering.

Following this the school children ran off to their school in anticipation to await their many and varied presents of sweets, goodies of all kinds and sports equipment such as footballs, rugby balls, tennis and squash racquets, etc. These gifts were to thank them and the villagers who supply flowers for all times of the year on the memorial and the graves behind their church where our boys lie. Naturally enough all the children wanted to sound and handle my silver bugle and were allowed to do so with myself keeping a tight hold on to the cord in case it was dropped. After this there was a reception in the village community hall where only our members were invited and once again we were offered champagne. By this time I was now getting quite accustomed to being hugged and kissed on both cheeks.

Later, some of us were again irresistibly drawn back for a last look and goodbye to the little cemetery behind the Church where we silently read the names on the gravestones of the boys we all knew, and before leaving I was asked if I would sound our regimental call, and believe me when I say that never before had it sounded so beautiful, so I did it twice. We left with heavy hearts after signing the Book of Remembrance and again noticed the bullet-ridden and marked walls on the south side of this picturesque little Church and the statue of Christ shot in half; the villagers have conserved this wanton destruction for all to see and ponder on.

Two days later we visited the town of Arras to which we had been invited and again we were welcomed with open arms and at the two war memorials I was again requested to sound the Last Post and Reveille with the townspeople and dignitaries gathered around. It was another solemn occasion after which everyone again assembled in the spacious town hall and again champagne was served in accordance with the French custom and I am now expert in the art of receiving kisses on both cheeks.

On the Friday, when we knew everyone had departed from the beaches of Dunkirk, we went back to talk and reminisce, to stand silently before the large memorial, and our minds took us back into history. Once again the German Stuka bombers dived and wheeled above us unleashing their screaming death bombs. Our own Bofors and anti-aircraft guns rattled off their five shells in rapid succession. Our naval ships pounded the terrain behind us with their huge guns and in the nearby proximity the German 109 fighter planes were setting up miniature sand storms with their never-ceasing machine-gunning. I remembered how helpless I was and must have resembled a very sorry and forlorn spectacle; naked except for dirty and soiled bandages and a 'T' and 'M' printed with my own blood on my forehead. ('T' for tourniquet and 'M' for morphine.) I again lay with others amongst the sand dunes whilst our hospital ship was being bombed and machine-gunned relentlessly whilst berthed at the old Mole (which by the way has now almost disappeared) and when danger came exceptionally close there was no shortage of willing bodies to help cover us from receiving further wounds. Our sense of smell once again remembered the acrid and pungent odours of the massive oil tanks and installations burning behind us, the crackle of flames and exploding material as vehicles and ships were bombed and blown to smithereens...Then a friend touched my arm and said, 'Come on Ernie, time to go.'

A short way along the coast at Bray Dunes our veteran Doctor Woolstone was also again applying his skills to the wounded at a small casualty post he had set up, whilst quite near to the Doc an old friend of mine, 'ginger' Futter, was still fighting back with all he had got until the enemy artillery guns got the range of the beach, but then again and fortunately for everyone, most of the shells buried themselves into the soft sand.

I am deeply conscious of the overwhelming fact and unshakable in the belief that our deliverance was masterminded by a great power, who calmed the seas for those very few days, after which, when no-one was left on the beaches, the wind was whipped up into a frenzy to gale force and the sea became mountainous and I was one of the very fortunate who was taken by the hand and can now say with great thankfulness, 'I saw the darkness put to flight – I saw the morning break.'

Did you know, in the *New York Times* on 1st June 1940, when reporting on the evacuation, were the truly appropriate words, 'The shining thing in the souls of free men is the great tradition of democracy – it is the future – it is the Victory.'

Our pilgrimage over and safely back home again, today I feel an uncontrollable uneasiness in my heart, when I think of the two previous World Wars and dwell on the fact that the great Berlin Wall is no longer

162

evident and a massive people is again undivided. I fervently pray to God that He will guide them along the true path of love and understanding.

I am well aware that many may wonder if I am a sentimental and compassionate old fool – well I am, unashamedly so, as are most old soldiers who have seen active service, and shortly I hope to prove this point to you, if our two lovely lady editors decide to print the true story of an animal which was a beast of burden whilst a friend of mine was fighting in the jungles of Burma. So, in the meantime, just hang on a little while for 'I remember... the Story of Oscar'. I'm sure you will like it.

The Story of 'Oscar'

I met Geoffrey about three years ago when on one of our trips to France and Belgium. Whilst in the Army he held the rank of Sergeant, and is now a member of the Burma Star Association, but regardless of which Regiment one served in we are all ex-comrades-in-arms, and I remember seeing him with tears in his eyes like the rest of us as we stood silently at the memorial in Le Paradis to honour the 97 men of the 2nd Bn. Royal Norfolk Regiment massacred there during 1940. Afterwards over a drink in our hotel in Belgium we swopped our many tales of experience during the war years, and when I met him again this year I asked him to repeat the full moving story of 'Oscar', which prompted me to tell you a short while back that most old soldiers who have seen active service with all its horrors are at heart unashamedly sentimental and compassionate in their everyday thinking.

During the middle of 1943 General Orde Wingate commanded a small force of Long Range Penetration Groups, who, for the first time since the Japanese had taken Burma and the neighbouring countries, had marched deep into enemy territory and inflicted considerable damage. More to the point, they had shown for all to see that British troops could beat the Japs at their own game.

So, back home again in India, Wingate decided that 1944 would see a second invasion of Japanese-held territory, but this time instead of just one brigade (normally made up of three regiments) he would have five brigades. Four would be flown in, and only one, on foot, would draw enemy fire and act as a kind of 'Aunt Sally' for the Japs to chase. Geoffrey was in the one

163

selected to march in, armed with light weapons, and a mile allocated to every ten men.

From mid-1943 the regiments selected to form the force and to be trained for Wingate's latest penetration were given training in every aspect of close combat fighting and equipment suited best for jungle use was developed and brought into the daily routine. Their clothing was modified until they were even dressed differently from other British troops, with green trousers, angola drab shirts, bush hats, double large packs modified by the local shoe repairers and equipped with Bren guns, Sten guns, American carbines, Mills hand-grenades, heavy machine guns, 2 inch and 3 inch mortars and portable flame-throwers known as 'Lifebuoys' because of their resemblance to the well-known safety aid. The force had to be christened for reasons of security and they became the 3rd Indian Division which was not very popular as included in the force were British, Burmese and African troops but no Indian force of any description. Later they acquired the title of 'Chindits', a corruption of the Burmese word 'Chinthe', the ceremonial beast guarding the entrance to every Burmese Pagoda, and this was later depicted within their Divisional Badge.

During training it was found that 'A' Category, the top medical grade, was not enough to ensure that troops were of sufficient staying power, and a new category of 'A plus' was enforced, weeding out many, and those who were re-categorised grew leaner and fitter as the extensive training went on.

Conversation at the normal level was forbidden as at times in the days ahead they could find themselves in close proximity to the enemy in very thick and overgrown jungle conditions found almost everywhere in Northern Burma and after a while their voices became almost non-existent and took weeks to recover once the fighting was over.

Navigation became a very important factor and many exercises were carried out at night using astral sightings. Geoffrey told me he could still remember most of the constellations they used even after a lapse of forty-six years.

Early in 1944 they joined a troop train taking them up to Assam and the Ledo Road; it was time for General Wingate to start his second expedition. They had progressed for only a few days when they came upon an Indian bullock in a small clearing. He was pale grey in colour with the usual rugby ball hump on his shoulders, and he looked a very handsome fellow indeed. It was at first thought this was a Jap ruse and booby trap, but no, he had been left behind by a column a few days ahead because of a badly poisoned flank, but they quickly scouted around just in case. To care for the mules and stretcher ponies a veterinary was attached to each column and the bullock was given an injection of whatever it is that vets inject sick animals with, and soon they had a lovely piece of reserve rations ambling and lolloping along the jungle tracks with them. He was apparently an amiable type of animal and boasted an enormous pair of horns of the type which Indian bullocks are adorned with, and when the column moved he moved, and when they rested he rested also. He became a constant companion to them all. After a short while their latest acquisition became known as 'Oscar', and soon they all became accustomed to seeing his slow deliberate ambling, which never seemed to vary although the mules seemed always to either shed their loads on steep slopes or to slither down and about on the slippery paths along the hillsides.

Apart from the back-breaking marching in single file from daybreak to sunset every day, their thoughts turned daily to the all important subject of the inner man – food. Each man was responsible for cooking his own meal and every five days a supply drop was, in theory, arranged, but alas, usually the parachutes ended up in an air stream which left rations three or more miles away in trees 80 feet high, and many were the times when the recovery rate was less than fifty per cent. All in all they were a hungry bunch, not of their choosing, gradually working their laborious, weary and hazardous journey along the Naga Hills.

An old engraving of a Brahmin Bull

165

They had been on the march for about a month, and at dawn on one morning they were informed that an overdue supply drop had again been postponed, and they had absolutely nothing left in their food packs in the way of eats, and there was no prospect of seeing a supply drop for at least two or more days. The time had come for emergency measures to be taken, and the order was passed down from Column H.Q. that Oscar would have to be killed. On this day, said Geoffrey, he had charge of Oscar, and in his section was a butcher by trade, named Bole Lester. Geoffrey says he will never forget that day as he gave an order for the butcher to kill and the man flatly refused, saying he could never eat Oscar and in any case he was not employed as a butcher whilst in the Army. The order was passed to the adjoining Section and they also refused, and the Sergeant in Charge passed it on to the next and so on all the way down the line. The order to kill Oscar went out to 450 starving men and not one of them would see him harmed. Everyone marched on for the next two days until the delayed drop arrived. Oscar seemed to have had an instinct that this column had cared for his welfare, and had adopted them as his own, whilst he roamed amongst them at will. When they halted he did so as well, and took his fill of whatever vegetation there was to offer, plus a good ration of the food which had been dropped by air for the mules and ponies, and when they moved off so did he, as much as if to tell them, 'You saved me, I like you and you're not going to leave me behind like that last lot did.' So there it was, deep in the heart of the Burmese jungle he had won the hearts of the whole unit, the tough, fearless and ruthless fighters trained to kill on sight or be killed.

Geoffrey believes that fate moves in a mysterious way – don't we all know this? – as later on in the campaign he was wounded in the thigh enough to paralyse his whole leg, and it was then impossible for him to walk, let alone march, bearing his equipment. All the hospital ponies were fully accounted for in stretchering the seriously wounded, and for a while it looked as if he would have to be left behind with a supply of ammunition and hand-grenades and if the Japanese did get to him before he could be picked up he would take as many of the enemy with him as was possible. And then they thought of Oscar; why could he not be fixed up as a temporary carrier? So with the help of a makeshift surcingle and blanket he was equipped as an ambulance carrier with Geoffrey on his back, and a short time later he also carried another wounded man with no difficulty whatsoever, and it appeared he was quite willing to do so.

Five days and nights passed by, interspersed with enemy attacks with mortars, machine guns and rifle fire, before they crept into the jungle stronghold fortress known as the White City. Oscar had helped in saving Geoffrey's life and had later gone back with the ponies to bring in a succession of wounded men before the Brigade was air-lifted out.

Geoffrey was recovering in hospital when he next saw Oscar – on film, as he was landed back in India by a DC3 (better known as a Dakota which could accommodate up to 22 stretcher cases plucked from almost inaccessible areas). He talked later with some of his men who told him that at the end of the operations the order was given to abandon all the animals in Burma and to evacuate troops only, but the muleteers were having none of this and more or less refused to leave them in the jungle to fend for themselves, and by the method known as 'The Ways and Means Act' the Army did eventually arrange a special pick-up by DC3s for all surviving mules and ponies and their drivers – and, of course, the animal which during the months of hardship and privation had become a companion to the whole unit, none other than Oscar.

It would have been nice to know how Oscar had fared on his return to India, but one thing is certain – he could never again receive the kindness and attention offered to him whilst on his trek through the dense jungle and heavy undergrowth which Burma had to offer; and for a few years yet to come there will still be tough old jungle fighters who think and talk about him as their four-legged friend with the long horns.

Coincidences

During 1944-45 I was still serving as a soldier in the Middle East (M.E.F.) and at the time was stationed in the Canal area of Egypt. I was fortunate to be in a privileged position, in which I had my own vehicle and travelled around the area, sometimes with an Arab interpreter and sometimes unaccompanied.

On one such occasion I was alone, travelling from Suez to Port Said along a road bordered by the Suez Canal on the east side and the lesser known Sweet Water Canal on the west. I first stopped for a 'spit and a draw' (old army slang for a smoke) at a place named Fayid on the side of the Great Bitter Lake. I then carried on up, passing through Ismailia and other places en route, and stopped again at El Quantara.

I immobilized my vehicle and was sitting on the sand beside the Canal bank, when my attention was drawn to the sudden violent rush of water towards the direction of Port Said, just as if someone had pulled the plug out. I looked in that direction, and there in the distance saw the huge superstructure of a massive ship. It was proceeding slowly and seemed to be taking up the whole width of the Canal. I had often seen other ships pass through the Canal, but never one such as this! I then realized it was a Royal Navy warship, and watched almost spell-bound as it approached, bristling with turrets of 14 and 16-inch guns. When it actually passed my position, the starboard side was so near to the edge of the Canal I could have leant over and actually touched it, and I saw sand and other debris being disturbed on the banks and sucked up by the air intakes.

Being of great length and massive proportions it took some minutes to pass, and salutations and back-chat were exchanged between the sailors and myself. Also, to my astonishment, I saw the name to be H.M.S. *King George V*, which at the time I knew to be one of our greatest and largest battleships. Naturally, having passed my position, all the water which had cascaded past to meet the oncoming ship now came swirling back in its wake, and with the huge screw propellers churning the bottom, most old ex-servicemen who remember the obnoxious odours of Egypt will understand fully when I say, I was prompted to resort to another 'spit and a draw'.

H.M.S. King George V

I must mention now that H.M.S. *King George V* was 45,173 tons, 745 feet in length, with a beam of 112 feet, and the Suez Canal was at the time 103 miles long and varied in width from 150-300 feet, but mostly it was only 150 feet wide. The depth was 26½ feet, with a bottom width of 72½ feet. The width did not allow the ship to veer very much, so what a brilliant feat of seamanship and navigation this was!

At times like this, secrecy enfolded the movements of naval vessels, and I could only know then that the ship would pass along the Canal, through the Bitter Lakes into the Gulf of Suez, to the Red Sea, and thence to the Indian Ocean. I have related my experience many times, and been met with scepticism and almost point-blank, 'Impossible, I can't believe it!' However, about eleven years on, I had exchanged one service for another, and was stationed at a quiet little village named Guist, with the church on a hill, about five miles from Fakenham. Here I met and became friendly with one, William (Billy) Fielding. Our friendship was immediately on, he being ex-Royal Navy and I ex-Army. We had lots to talk about. After a while I ventured to relate my story to him, and he listened intently and without interruption, and when I had finished I waited for the usual derisive remarks, but instead he said, 'Do you know, you have made my day! I served on *George V* and vividly remember our trip through the Suez Canal.' He corroborated what I have just told you. He further went on to tell me that following the voyage through the Canal, where the ship had been so near to the sides, the air intakes had indeed taken in excessive sand and debris, as I had seen. Sand had found its way into the engine room, and other damage had been caused to the hull and keel.

Now comes the added coincidence. On reaching a pre-arranged port the ship had to undergo minor repairs and a clean-up, and whilst in dry dock electricity was supplied by ship-to-ship cable from a Royal Navy submarine which had been floated alongside. Billy was leaning over the rail of his ship when a heavy hand slapped him on the shoulder and a voice said, 'Billy, what ....' (This I cannot quote!) It turned out to be a sailor off the submarine who lived in the small village of Wood Norton, not a mile from Foulsham where Billy lived, and they knew each other very well.

During my frequent visits to Port Said I often sat at the foot of the statue of the French engineer, Ferdinand de Lesseps, who built the Canal, looking out to the Mediterranean, with thoughts of home. 'Aha! But...' I can imagine some of you saying, 'that fool E.J.L. has got his facts in a twist; too many years in the blazing sun in the land of the Pharaohs must have got at him!' For, my friends, when you recently travelled through the Suez Canal, of course you didn't see Ferdinand at Port Said, and the Canal seemed and looked much wider than this fool said it is –150 feet wide at its narrowest points, indeed! – but, in 1956 the Egyptians took the old boy away to pastures new, and at the same time widened the narrow points to 196 feet 10 inches. So there!

I must tell you that after her journey, *King George V* served with U.S.A. ships in the Pacific during the Okinawa campaign, and bombarded the Japanese facilities in the Ryukyu islands. She was also in Tokyo Bay on 2nd September, 1945, for the Japanese surrender. Earlier, she fired the last salvos which finally sunk the heroic Germans and their battleship *Bismarck* in that historic chase and sea battle.

Thanks for sharing this with me – but, tell me, why is a ship called 'she'? Surely this is most impolite when one is named H.M.S. *King George V*, H.M.S. *Nelson* or *Rodney*, etc.?

The R101, the Pride of Britain's Airship Fleet

In 1924 the British Imperial Defence Committee commenced a considerable construction programme building airships, and plans were drawn up for an airship service for the Empire route to India via Egypt, where tethering masts were put up at Ismailia. In consequence two airships were built – the R101 and her sister ship the R100, commencing on 14th October 1929. Both were built at Cardington, Bedfordshire. Much of the aluminium and steel strutting was manufactured at the Norwich riverside factory of Boulton and Paul.

After being built, the R101 was 732 feet long with a diameter of 131 feet, and had five 650 horse power Beardmore Tornado diesel engines underslung to give tremendous power. During the maiden flight it was found that its weight was considerably greater than first calculated and

171

another 44 feet was added to her. The total length was now 776 feet, or 258 and a bit yards – what a monster! It was estimated that after this modification she had cost the British taxpayer over £1,000,000 but even then she had not been tested for bad weather conditions or at full speed, and it is said, and on record, that some engineers had grave doubts. However, she would now accommodate 100 passengers, carry a full volume of 5,500,000 cubic feet of hydrogen gas and had a flight range of 3,600 to 5,000 miles. The then Lord Thompson, Secretary of State for Air during 1930, pronounced her as safe as a house except for the millionth chance.

On Saturday, 4th October 1930, during the evening, she took off from her moorings at Cardington with 54 passengers and crew on board. About 600 feet over the Channel she pitched and rolled through rainstorms, was buffeted by winds of 40-50 knots when somewhere off the N.W. coast of France, and according to eyewitnesses she flew only 300 feet above the ground at Abbeville. At 2.05 hours on Sunday, 5th October 1930 the R101 started to go down by nose and the officer handling the elevator controls struggled to keep her on an even keel; water ballast was jettisoned but all attempts to reach height proved to be futile. Three minutes later at 2.08 hours the airship dived into a slight rise near Beauvais and in a few seconds over 5,000,000 cubic feet of hydrogen gas became an inferno, no doubt after contact with hot engines or red hot exhaust pipes. Only four men survived, when water tanks split open and doused the flames around them. The R101 had been the pride and joy of the British airship fleet, and the conflagration, which turned her into the tangled and crumpled mass, saw the whole nation into a state of mourning.

Now, I know what you are thinking: 'Why ever is he rambling on about the largest airship ever built, even if it was British?' Well, I will try to enlighten you.

I was just over ten years of age in 1930 and sometimes couldn't get out of bed until the last minute on schooldays, in which case there was not time for breakfast. So I needed a walk between one telegraph pole and a fast run between the next two to cover the one-and-a-half miles to Fleggburgh School. I cannot define the day or date, but I think in the early days of the first week of October 1930 I was already late for school when, on reaching the corner at High House Farm, Billockby where the pit used to be on the side of the road, I heard the most unusual and unfamiliar droning in the sky behind me from the direction of the marshes and river. On looking back over South Farm House, Clippesby, I saw an amazing sight the like of which I had never seen before and was never to witness again. I stood as if spellbound, unable to move on, and just watched as this massive cigar-shaped airship flew past over the marshes less than a mile away. I was able to see the large black lettering G-FAAW on the body, a 'G' on the rudder fin and R101 at the nose and tail. I had heard and read about airships but when I saw this massive dark silver-grey leviathan in the sky I just could not believe my eyes. It was as if I had not yet woken up. And about ten minutes later the schoolmaster, Mr Tweddell, could not believe his ears. I rushed into the classroom where some giggled and others grimaced because they knew what was to come. The Head looked at me and in a quiet voice said, 'Late again, James,' and I blurted out what I had seen, but his eyes from behind his spectacles took on the most incredulous look of disbelief, and I knew then that I was in for it.

There are still some of us left who can remember our classroom, the fireplace in the corner with the head's desk near to it and, facing the class, the glass-fronted cupboard near the wall to the left where on one shelf nothing was ever placed for it was used solely to house the instrument which we all hated, namely the thin, slender cane. I held out both hands as he thrashed me, three on each palm, he said as if counting the strokes up to six, 'A most incredible and inappropriate excuse.' The tears stung my eyes; not so much because of the pain, but to think I was being punished for telling the truth. I could not hold my pen to write down my lessons and had to catch up, losing my playtime breaks on the following days until finished. Much to my vexation I had to resort to a dictionary to find out the meaning of the words which the head had used. Later I took and showed him a cutting from the paper which said that the airship had flown over Norfolk, and I was told that Norfolk was a large county and even if I had been punished wrongly I could count it as an adjustment for getting away with other misdemeanours in the past.

In the *News of the World* and other papers on the Sunday there were full front pages entirely devoted to the crash and showing photographs of the huge frame lying in a tangled and twisted mass on the ground, and I kept telling myself that I had seen this massive and impressive airship pass over near to me in all its short-lived glory, but I could not prove it, and it niggled at the back of my mind.

And now, sixty years on, I was driving over to Clippesby one Sunday afternoon early this year, listening to Radio Norfolk. I had on previous Sundays heard Mr Ralph Tuck, a freelance broadcaster, giving very

173

interesting talks on various rural and steam engineering subjects, and much to my delight his subject was now about airships moored at Pulham in Norfolk and Cardington in Bedfordshire. He mentioned the R101 having flown on a proving flight from Cardington and crossing over Sandringham where the Royal Family were in residence, and then over the home of the Aviation Minister of the time, Sir Samuel Hoare, who lived at North Repps. It then flew over Boulton and Paul's factory at Norwich, as they were involved in some items in its construction, and then it flew over Pulham which at that time was an R.A.F. airship station.

I wrote to Ralph Tuck informing him of my schoolboy story, asking if he could confirm my sighting of the airship on that memorable morning. I am most pleased and thankful that he wrote back to me quoting the facts in the previous paragraph, and also calling my attention to a book called 'The Pulham Pigs' which embraced the airship progress of the day on the airfield at Pulham and which I did eventually manage to obtain from the library and read with avid interest. Ralph Tuck also wrote, 'Like you, as a small boy I stood in the playground at Burston Primary School and saw the R101 go over after it had flown over Pulham, on its way back to Cardington in Bedfordshire.'

I have long since forgiven my headmaster as I realize on that morning in October 1930 I saw a spectacle which was engraved into the history books for all time. And perhaps if any of you have doubts, and wish to agree with Mr Tweddell about the credibility of this story, then just for the heck of it, please get out your maps of Norfolk and a ruler and draw a line from North Repps to the eastern side of Norwich. This will give you just a rough flightpath taken by the largest and most expensive airship ever built, and which I had the good fortune to see. If your conscience troubles you, please apologize the next time we meet!

A Pilgrimage of Sorrow

On Saturday, 28th May, 1988, the Dunkirk Veterans from all over the U.K. left our native shores once again for France and Belgium, to pay respects to those of our comrades who lost their lives there in 1940, and my own Norfolk and Norwich branch left Dover and arrived in France to begin our pilgrimage during the early afternoon. We had an hotel in Dunkirk and on the next day, Sunday, there was a massive parade and march past in the town centre. Those persons whom I constantly overhear saying, 'The French and Belgians do not care,' should at sometime in their lives attend one of these parades and take note of the thousands of French and Belgians who still acutely remember and care.

The parade was followed by a service at the Allied Memorial on the beach, during which many memories were relived. The two minutes' silence enabled me to remember vividly how as a young soldier of 20 years I lay on the beach seriously wounded, naked except for bandages and covered with a blanket, with the incessant screaming of bombs and shells, gunfire and the mind-shattering noises of war, unable to fend for myself when every minute danger threatened, comrades unknown to me shielded me with their own bodies. The time seemed endless, and lying in the part-shelter of the sand dunes, I welcomed the varied visits of the M.O. and the soothing relief of morphine. The bugler sounding Reveille aroused each of us from bygone nightmares. It was a most moving service, and after the wreaths were laid, we from Norfolk placed poppy crosses on the water line to be eventually washed away by the tide.

From the beaches where the old Mole can just be discerned above the water line, we moved on to the British Memorial, where again emotions could not be effectively contained. The many tablets told us of the boys who did not return home, and on one were the names and numbers of four boys of the 2nd Royal Norfolks with whom I had been in constant close contact from 1935 to 1940, and unfortunately for whom there is no known grave. Whilst there I located the grave of Harry Woolston who as a schoolboy lived at Billockby, and was one of my school friends and playmates. Harry made it to within 21 miles of our homeland coast before he died, and once again I was brought to remember how I gained consciousness somewhere on the south coast, Newhaven I believe, being gently shaken by a beautiful young Sally Army Nurse, who said to me, 'Welcome home, you are safely back in England!'

I can endorse everything that has been said and written of the memorials and burial grounds for our forces in France and Belgium. They are indeed spotlessly clean and tidy, the churches and grounds are beautifully kept and litter-free. The headstones are set in grassy lawns, bordered with gardens and filled with flowers. May I also tell you that when we left, after suffering the tramping of thousands of feet, the grounds were still as beautiful and litter-free as we had found them.

175

On the Monday, thousands gather at Le Paradis. For those not familiar with what occurred, I will explain briefly. It was desperate and 'A', 'B' and 'C' companies were virtually non-existent, and 'D' company was surrounded. The German casualties were extremely heavy and their attack subsided. This punishment and the delay it caused may well have infuriated the German S.S. which led to the crime that was to follow. Meanwhile H.Q. Company was holding out at Duries Farm, Le Paradis. Under shell-fire the farm was set ablaze, ammunition was exhausted and after showing a white flag, which at first was ignored, nearly 90 men gathered outside the farm, including the wounded brought up from the cellars, and were taken prisoners by men of the German 1st Bn. 2nd S.S. Totenkopt Regiment. Their weapons were taken from them and on order from an officer were marched along Rue du Paradis to an open paddock, and as they marched through a gateway past the wall of a long barn, two machine guns opened up from the back of a truck and the column of men was mown down. Those still alive were finished off by revolver shots and bayonet thrusts. A plaque on the still-visible battle-scarred wall of the barn tells of this massacre. Here again a short service was held, and we five from the Regiment were given the prominent position at the front. Again during the two minutes' silence our dulled senses were alive to the ominous splutter of the machine guns, and I hung my head with tears burning my eyes, not wishing my distress to be witnessed. After a few seconds I raised my head and on glancing along our line saw my friends were in the same state as myself, with uncontrollable tears streaming down their faces, but not only us, everyone around us was having the same difficulty.

From the barn we moved on to the Church where, because of the size of the crowds attending, the service was relayed by loudspeaker to those outside. After this came the laying of wreaths on our own memorial immediately outside the Church. The people of Le Paradis gave us the plot of land on which it stands, and in return we keep in touch and supply the children attending school there with sweets, etc. The memorial is also cleaned by them and flowers are placed there all the year round.

Next came the most emotional period of our pilgrimage, in visiting the graves in the little cemetery behind the Church where our own were at rest next to the civilian cemetery. Can you just imagine our distress; everyone whose name appeared with the regimental crest, had been known to us, and as I lingered with my friend, ex-Capt. Walter Gilman, we stood for a brief moment in front of each one of them. Being the last two to leave the cemetery we were joined by a Scottish piper who at his own bidding piped for us the 'Lament'.

On leaving this very special place we saw the battle-scarred face of the east wall to the Church with its shattered and bullet-ridden statue of Christ; the villagers had voted unanimously to leave it just as it had happened. Again the cemetery was immaculate and tidy, and scrupulously clean and orderly. The people really do care.

This has been written to coincide with Armistice Sunday, when exhortations will be voiced around an untold number of memorials, and may I say, with the greatest respect, there is one in a far off distant land where the epitaph reads:

'WHEN YOU GO HOME, TELL THEM OF US AND SAY:
FOR YOUR TOMORROW WE GAVE OUR TODAY.'

Could I just mention – I have a very clear photograph of the grave of Harry Woolston, showing all details. If any of his relatives should read this magazine and wish to have a photograph, one will be given. Also, God willing, I shall be visiting Dunkirk and Le Paradis again in another year, and anyone who has a loved one in either of these cemeteries and would treasure a photograph of his grave, I will gladly oblige.

Memorial at Le Paradis

177

Postscript: Jimmy's brother, Freddie

Freddie Leggett was known to everyone in the Fleggs and regarded with much affection and admiration. He was a very remarkable man, out and about in all weathers in his wheelchair despite being paralysed in the spine and unable to use his legs. He died in 1986.

Freddie fought hard to overcome his disability. He looked after himself, his cottage, his garden, his livestock and his neighbours. He went fruit-picking each summer and he was a very fine shot. Besides all this he had a paper delivery round in Burgh, Billockby and Clippesby for over fifty years – unfailingly rising at 6.30am six days of the week. His fortitude was a splendid example to all.

Memories of Freddie

Eastern Daily Press/Archant

'My first meeting with Freddie Leggett almost twenty years ago was when he arrived at the house to give me the most beautiful bunch of flowers grown in his garden as a welcome-to-Billockby present. Every day since then Freddie has delivered the newspapers and we all miss the familiar sound of his invalid car at

8 o'clock every morning. Freddie was always cheerful with a very ready smile and always took a great interest in the children and dogs and every day he gave our two labradors a piece of bread when he delivered the papers.

All the people in the village feel a great loss. Freddie did so many kind deeds for everyone, shopping, collecting pensions to name but a few. In his leisure time he went to the field around the church and shot rabbits, this he also did in harvest time if he could manage to get in a field near the combine. We will all miss Freddie as people of his character and general view of life are few and far between.'
M.M.Alston

'Some years ago Freddie was in hospital for some months. Whilst he was away I took over his paper round, and very soon discovered the hard work he did for the villagers every single day. Collecting pensions, postal orders, stamps, groceries, meat etc., and sometimes pills and medicines from the doctor.'
Sheila Tooke

'Freddie was always very generous. Nothing was too much trouble. He would always help anyone. A first class man and one who really overcame disabilities that would have put down lesser men.'
Horace Claxton

'...he was a good and faithful friend, who'd enjoy a 'natter' and also love to spoil our dog, as he did many other animals.'
Gill and Billy Barker

'...nothing but praise for the wonderful work Freddie did over the many years he worked for the Post Office at Fleggburgh.'
Jake Clarke

'Freddie was a friend to all – the children chatted to him outside the shop and loved to climb inside his little blue car. Many times he would give them a few pennies to get themselves some sweets... Freddie is now part of Fleggburgh and the surrounding hamlets' history, a character who gave so much of himself when his life had more limitation than most.'
Post Office Stores, Fleggburgh

'We could not let Freddie Leggett pass away without paying our tribute to him. He was a man of remarkable character – never once have we heard him grumble or complain.'
Nellie Gowing

'Freddie was a good cook and if you went round to his house at 5 p.m. there was always an appetising smell. He liked his pigeon pie. He would skin, not pluck his pigeons. He always had plenty of vegetables in his garden, he had lots of flowers too, especially at the Harvest Festival time with his prize chrysanthemums. He used to supply each of the two local churches with flowers. He used to take chickens in to Acle market in his old three-wheeler chair cranking it all the way to Acle and back with boxes of chickens on the platform in front and everywhere. He would do this up to four times each Thursday at peak periods.'
Janet Starking

'Mr Jack Key gave Freddie permission to shoot over his land when and where he pleased. He himself remembers him so well with 'Pud' Hudson (nobody can remember his Christian name), rabbiting in the fields Freddie travelling in his little box. He always thinks too, of the evenings when the three of them used to go to Billockby Reading Room to play cards. Freddie in his little box which was left outside the door, and he used to scramble in and climb on to his stool. After he had his chair, he and 'Pud' used to go to the pictures in Yarmouth. 'Pud' having lost a foot was also disabled at this time. They were treated very kindly at the picture house.

The little box was a wooden box with sides about six inches high, with a little wheel each side, propelled by Freddie pushing a stick on to the ground. When his pals came home from school or work they would fix a piece of cord to the front of the box and pull him, sometimes with hazardous results, but he always came up smiling.'
Reggie Key

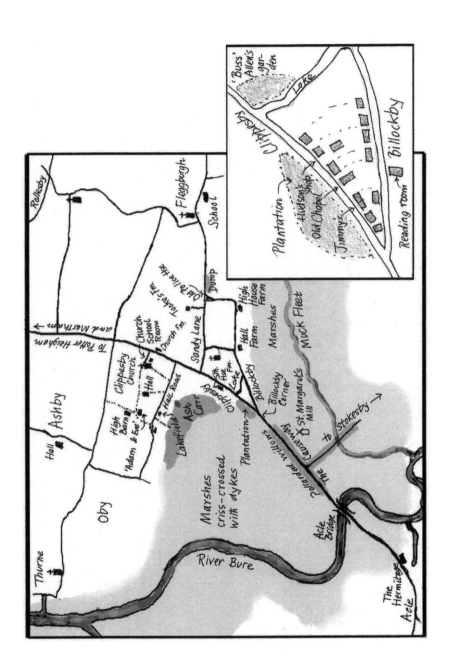

Buss' Allen's garden

Lake

Clippesby

Billockby

Plantation

Hudson's Shop

Old Chapel

Jimmy's

Reading room

Rollesby

Fleggburgh

School

To Potter Heigham and Martham →

Oby Lane Ho.

Teacher's Ho.

Dump

High House Farm

Church School Room

Church Fm.

Sandy Lane

Hall Farm

Marshes

Muck Fleet

Ashby

Clippesby Church

Hall

Sh. Hse. Fm. Cafe

Billockby

Billockby Corner

St. Margaret's Mill

→ to Stokesby

High Barn

'Adam & Eve'

Hall Road

Lakefield

Ash Carr

Clippesby

Plantation →

The Willows

Pollard Causeway

Acle Bridge

Hall

Oby

Marshes criss-crossed with dykes

River Bure

Thurne

The Hermitage

Acle